New
&
Selected Poems

To my great-grandchildren

New
&
Selected Poems

Ruth Bidgood

seren

Seren is the book imprint of
Poetry Wales Press Ltd
Nolton Street, Bridgend, Wales, CF31 3BN
www.seren-books.com

The right of Ruth Bidgood to be identified as the
Author of this Work has been asserted in
 accordance with the Copyright, Designs
and Patents Act, 1988.

ISBN 1-85411-377-1

A CIP record for this title is available from the British
Library.

The publisher acknowledges the financial assistance
of the Welsh Books Council.

Printed by CPD (Wales), Ebbw Vale

Contents

from *The Given Time* (1972)

from *Not Without Homage* (1975)

from *Lighting Candles* (1982)
(new poems section)

from *Kindred* (1986)

from *Selected Poems* (1992)
(new poems section)

from *The Fluent Moment* (1996)

from *The Given Time* (1972)

The Given Time

That could have been my time –
The years to come, all meaning gone
From the broken shape of the house,
Blurred like a thicker shadow
Than tree-shadows in the silent forest;
Hardly a shape even – a darkness,
Irregularity, among the ordered trees –
Not a memory left, not a line of its story.

But in this time decreed as mine,
With hardly a stone yet fallen, the house is lapped
By the first waves of forest-land
Whose crests bear the tiny trees.
The house has lost its life, not yet identity –
It is known hereabouts, stories are still told
Of men who lived there. Silent, it poses questions,
Troubles me with half-answers, glimpses, echoes.

To accept as mine this given time,
To live the haunted present and know the forest's shadow,
Is the one way to break from snatching branches,
And back over nursery furrows stumble at last
To where in the winds of the past the house rose whole,
A shape of life in a living valley –
Winter brightening the low rooms
With snow-light and spark-spattering logs,
Or spring's shadows playing like lambs,
Racing with the sun like children over the fields.

Chimneys

Far away, we saw three chimneys in the trees
Across the valley, on a little hill
Beyond the first hill's shoulder.

Shading our eyes from the sidelong evening sun,
We gazed and guessed till we could almost see
The roofs of beast-house, stable and barn.

No smoke rose from the chimneys, we said at first,
But soon we swore there was smoke, so alive the house
Seemed in the dying sunlight.

And afterwards, alone, I searched on maps
To make the house more mine by knowing its name –
And found there is no farm on the hill,

No house of any kind, not even a ruin.
What trick of sun and shade put chimneys there
For us to find and talk about?

And is the evening more real than the house?
Now both are gone, it seems a fine distinction
That one was and the other was not.

Remembering, I build the evening again,
The plunging valley and the little hill,
And look! there are chimneys in the trees.

Distance

Over the golden hill on a still day
Swelled the blue summer-flood of sky;
And on that high tide buzzards floated,
So far away, their lonely crying
Was only a tiny sound with no emotion,
And their broad soaring and gliding hardly a ripple
In the ocean-firmament.
On the shore of the sky, the hill-horizon,
The blue surge broke in a froth of wild horses,
Luminous-maned, their galloping
Stylized by distance to a line of foam.
Now I am distant from that August day
The crying of the heart is far and tiny;
And shall I say that memory is lying,
Recording me as tranquil as the day?

Little of Distinction

Little of distinction, guide-books had said –
A marshy common and a windy hill;
A renovated church, a few old graves
With curly stones and cherubs with blind eyes:
Yews with split trunks straining at rusty bands:
And past the church, a house or two, a farm,
Not picturesque, not even very old.
And yet, the day I went there, life that breaks
So many promises, gave me a present
It had not promised – I found this place
Had beauty after all. How could I have seen
How a verandah's fantastic curlicues
Would throw a patterned shadow on the grass?
Or thought how delicate ash-leaves would stir
Against a sky of that young blue? or know
Trees and grey walls would have such truthful beauty
Like an exact statement? And least of all
Could I have foreseen the miles on hazy miles
Of Radnorshire and Breconshire below,
Uncertain in the heat – the mystery
That complements precision. So much sweeter
Was this day than the expectation of it.

Roads

No need to wonder what heron-guarded lake
Lay in the other valley,
Or regret the songs in the forest
I chose not to traverse.
No need to ask where other
              roads might have led,
Since they led elsewhere;
For nowhere but this here and now
Is my true destination.
The river is gentle in the soft evening,
And all the steps of my life have
              brought me home.

Shepherd's Cottage

In this window is no glass, no hindrance
To the thin wind, nothing to blur
Inhuman clarity of curlew's call,
Or lamb's cry despairing of answer,
Or water's small cold endless song.
It is long since peat or wood smoke rose
From the black hearth. There is nothing now
For windbreak hawthorn to shelter,
Nothing for rowan to protect.
This roof, these walls are losing what men gave;
Each year makes them more a mountain thing,
Impersonal, appropriate. But today
I lean on the sill, seeing what they saw
Who lived here, hearing what they heard;
And memory plays tricks, reminding me
Of things I cannot have known –
A girl's laugh as she looks back mockingly,
Climbing the loft ladder: bleat of a cade lamb
Fed by the fire; and voices of children,
Voices of children. Then the stream again,
The curlew's voice and the wind's; the rest are quiet.

Manor House

Do not reject this fading house
And say its beauty suits a decadent taste.
Much is dying here, but to miss the swan-song
Keeps nothing alive, blasphemes against the moment.

Do not reject this dying house.
It is as lovely over the field of thistles
And crowded round by too-heavy trees
As one a traveller came to years ago
And found the lawns lit with Lent lilies,
The sundial unbroken telling an old time
At the heart of the weedless garden,
And the boys gone squirrel-hunting in the woods.

Carreg-y-Frân

Here, where the deep track leads to tumbled walls
And a white scatter of sheep-bones, was the farm
With the best oats in these valleys – oats admired,
Coveted, bragged of, not yet quite forgotten.
The slumbering beast-backs of old hedges,
Crested with thorn-stumps, still mark the fields.
Cornishmen lodged here, bringing their expertise
To the lead-mine far up the gusty valley,
Where something creaks rustily on the silence.
All these years after, there is still a strangeness
In saying "The Cornishmen lived here" – their legend
Is simply that – they brought a foreignness,
Being self-sufficient, unpredictable
And strange in speech. The mine itself
Was alien, till it died. Now it is one
With a pattern of old fields stamped on the hill,
And roof-tiles lying splintered in the grass.

Turner's Painting of Hafod

The delicate fantastic house
Gleaming in sidelong light
Seems more alive yet less substantial
Than the foreground's romantic tangle
Of rocks, trees, and cascades,
Or the looming mass of hills behind.
Straight lines and balanced arches
Define the fragile body
Of one man's threatened dream
Amid the swirling grandeur of chaos.
The painter, prescient, saw the house
As if, its doom accomplished,
Already it haunted the valley and men's minds –
Hafod, luminous as its own legend.

Old Pump House, Llanwrtyd Wells

The door is open. I shall not be intruding,
Going in to sit on the bench by the wall,
To breathe the stuffy dankness streaked with sulphur,
And stare though broken panes over the shaggy grounds.
This sociable place has died through lack of visiting.
A pungent drip, still slowly forced from the spring's heart,
Has grown a fungus-garden in the great mirrored basin.
Some chairs lie on the sheep-fouled floor,
Some lurch, still conversationally grouped,
Against the counter over which was handed
Health by the tumblerful when crowds came here
Laughing and garrulous, to take the waters;
Pulling faces over the taste of their cure,
And bragging of the glasses they had drunk
Like boys about their beer. They came streaming
Six times a day from the bursting village
To jostle and gossip round the sulphur-bar.
Sheep-farmers, knitting wives, holiday miners
From the black valleys, jam-packed the houses,
Ate meals in shifts, and sat outside singing hymns
On the suddenly hushed street of evening;
Or went back in warm dusk to the well-house
To hear the Builth harper play under summer trees
And watch the youngsters dance.
The plucked notes, never wholly gay, and laughing voices
Spiralled up through the trees, up the long valley;
And lost themselves among the hills
Over the sealed frontier of the past.

Small Town Afternoon

In the square dazed with summer afternoon
bees hum high up in window-boxes,
tubs of flowers stand by doorsteps
and under striped awnings; even
the fourway signpost is rooted in an urn of flowers.
Old men watch through pipe-haze
smooth fish-shapes of holiday cars
slide in, check, glide from the pool of quiet.

A girl is telephoning in the hothouse box
sun insistent through this burning-glass
on flushed face and heavy yellow hair.
She pushes the door a little open
to dilute the stuffy prisoned heat
with that other heat of out-of-doors,
tainted with petrol and redeemed by flowers,
and laughs in answer to a laugh
across fifty miles of summer air.

Nant-y-Cerdin

In high morning I am haunted
        by long-ago mornings –
And even those were ghost-ridden
        by a more distant morning,
never quite remembered
        but never dying at noon.
Today when wheatears
        flash from sunny rocks
and new loose-limbed lambs
stagger appalled through the stony stream
        after stolid ewes;
when daffodils blow in the nettle-garden
        of a farm with broken windows,
and in a remote brown valley
the clammy standing stone
        grows warm to touch –
even today ghosts come
        whispering of a ghost.
Could there ever be a morning unhaunted,
a spring shining
        with no sunlight but its own?
Only the first, perhaps,
        the lost ideal morning,
the one that must be found,
must be lived or haunt me always,
the lost morning on forgotten hills.

Cefn Cendu

The furthest mountains lay like cloud
on the cloudless afternoon;
oaks billowed far below
round an island of intenser green.
From the slack-hung gate, the path
narrowed by fern led down
to a tree-bordered grassland shelf
high above the summer-heavy valley.
Suddenly, I saw the house.
I would never have wished its life away,
never have willed it to withdraw
into such silence. One beauty died
when the last owner, leaving, shut the door
and heard for the first time an echo
follow him from empty rooms.
Yet, as though the place held a will to beauty,
it had won kindness even from age
and dereliction, that had brought only
moss to the cobbles in the stable-yard,
grass to the gabled roof, and a stillness
that caught the breath.
I will not betray the vision I had of it,
will not recant, though now
after three years I have come back
in spring rain and found
trees cut down, cobbles lost
in rank grass, doors and windows gaping,
floor fouled and roof-tiles crumbling.
The house, once busy and ordinary,
is in its ruin ordinary again,
and stripped of secrets as of shade.
Yet the beauty I saw three years ago
is no less real for being hidden
behind a curve of the hill or turn of the years.
The path that leads to vision leads also away.

Log Fire

"Come to the fire," say my friends,
moving books and knitting from the settle.
Then I know I am back
after all the hours and miles,
and we sit in a sun-cave
all heat and brightness.

Light springs from logs, spreads from lamps,
beats back from a wall of brasses –
a charm of light against death-wish darkness
of the upper valley. From the window here,
through tossing boughs we lose and find
one light from the one house braced against wind
laden with snow from the black mountain
that rears twin cairns above a cataract few visit,
in a cold kingdom of black bog and rock.

Men, borderers of such a wilderness,
move on old ritual paths
through predictable seasons.
Faith piled these logs
against the sure coming of snow,
and is now vindicated as the first flakes fall
powerless to chill this warm creation, this evening
on the edge of desolation.

Cardiganshire Story

The baby died, of course,
his first night was his last.
Night was the murderer,
using all its weapons for the kill.
One would have done, the cold
on those hills, but night made sure,
using rain to soak the ragged blanket,
wind to drive home the cold and wet,
moonless dark to make the pony stumble
jolting the weak newborn,
stabbing the girl with pain,
pain and remembered pain,
drying her milk with fear.

Jogging and slithering through blackness,
mocked by an unseen river,
she clutched with one hand clammy reins,
with the other her damply-swaddled child,
afraid to let him fall, afraid not to,
afraid to bring him out of night
after the months of hiding and lies,
to morning light at her mother's house.

The river went on laughing
and voices spun giddily
telling her a river could wash away
a year, drown all its secrets –
saying Who would know, who?–
ride home alone, let him sleep, sleep.
But the child on her arm cried weakly
and she held him closer,
riding homewards in the lessening dark,
lurching dizzily as the path went down
out of the hills and the night to her mother's door.

The baby died, of course,
but night was the only murderer,
a killer with excessive strength
and no motive whatsoever.

Drowned Valley

I walk in a valley where under water
have gone houses, hayfields, walls men patched,
gates they hung, intransigent
rushy pieces they would carp at,
sweet land that reconciled them.
These things are gone beyond my sight
that knows only the present,
only the lake blue in precarious summer,
hills that once were hill-tops,
and one ruined farm, no longer high
on a hillside, but fortress-like
beside a beach with no seaweed, no gulls,
yet a scent a little like the sea.

Morning so young denies nostalgia;
could all drowned individual things
be now summed up, not lost,
in a grand generality of sky and water?
And yet – what in this classic beauty
expresses Ianto's crook-back or his smile?
What now includes the sidelan field
where the lame piebald grazed?
or Mari's cottage, with the oven-door askew?
The living eccentricities still hide
in their own time, lost to me, far and lost.
I read a phrase, but lack the all-including sentence;
the lake has no words but its own to say.

The Crow

The crow died ludicrously,
banging against a bough,
flopping untidily to ground,
dying in my hands –
beak opening as if thirsty,
eyes' fragile blinds
half-drawn to disown the world.

One less crow to peck lambs' eyes out
was hardly matter for grief;
yet any loud warm life
was hard to spare in the quiet wood
of weakly trees that put out fleshy frills
of fungus by a black morass
glutting huge rhododendrons.

Death, many-named, I name you now
breaker of images. You show me
my king crow – carrion-plunderer,
corn-ravager, harsh omen
cawing of fate at sickroom windows –
toppling down, victim after all,
a loser blundering to a silly end.

Stone

Arcadia was never here.
Ice-needles tortured the thin soil,
spring snow lay long by the north wall,
yet the peat-fire had a summer heart.
Waves of life receding left
jetsam of stone – grey megaliths
half-sunk in tussocky grass now
but still processional on the ridge above,
leading into a mystery:
in a cranny of the valley, a ring of stones
that sheltered a hearth once; a roofless hut
of later years, perched high upstream
under the shadow of cairned hills.
The rushes cut each autumn
to mend the thatch, one year
were cut no more; over the centuries
the path was lost. Only stone lasts here.
Stone proclaims life, affirms a future
by virtue of so many pasts,
yet baffles questioning. As I touch walls
warm in the sun today, and feel
so many summers gentle to my hand
and yet withheld, I would crush stone
in my fist, if I could, till truth's milk ran.

Hennant

Unguessed at half a field away,
under the slope by a hidden stream
foot-high walls have given in
to green encroachment – a tree grows
out of each corner of the house,
rank grass fills room and byre. The silence here
is one with all silence of broken places –
a barrier holding back the voices
that whisper and scream behind it.
To find this place, so suddenly, is to see
an old city rise from jungle, and to know
the silence that no shouting of birds can break
in the Hall of a Thousand Columns.

The courts of Chichen-Itza, where stone serpents
lurk in the grass, fantasticate
the plain verse of these dwindled walls
into a hundred intricate stanzas.
The sadness is the same, for what is not,
and triumph for what has been.
Stones are memorials, but in their disarray
and littleness against green wilderness
speak of beginnings, a new balance to strike,
not here perhaps, nor in the Ball Court
by the sacrificial pool.

On unforeseen slopes by a distant river
the walls that rise will be these walls;
and from the unimaginable future,
voices far from the Mayan jungle
murmur and shriek behind the silence
even now, in the echoing Ball Court
and the Hall of a Thousand Columns.

Malcontent

You, never satisfied with the rose you see,
never accepting the dry denial of stone,
or limitation in love – so, inevitably, alone –
spoilt child who cannot compromise or agree;

only, perhaps, at the feared and destined close
of all neat possibilities will you, blind,
see through the rock spring-water, find
the kiss that was never given and the impossible rose.

Passer-By

On a road by a slow river under a pewter sky,
from the car-window suddenly I saw a girl
who hand-in-hand with her lover walked exalted
in a first hour or last of happiness, it seemed.
The birth of her memory tore me too – I saw
as she would see, many years hence, these fields,
squat osiers crouched by the grey stream, and the four elms
towering from the flat land and indecipherably
presaging the outcome. And my face too
she would remember, momentarily turned to hers
in recognition of such vulnerability.

Spiders

She played the piano sometimes in the summer,
when westering sunlight through the open window
gave tarnished candlesticks and dusty curtains
a gentle elegance, so that not to age,
not to fade, would have seemed a lapse of taste.
The hesitant arpeggios, broken trills,
brought great shy listeners from the creepered trellis.
Scuttle and pause, scuttle and pause, came spiders
on tentative delicate legs, to hear the music;
and I, a child, stayed with them, unafraid –
till turning from the yellow keys, one day
she told me of a room where long ago
it had been she who saw the spiders drawn
helpless by threads of music, and listened with them.
Then I felt shut with her into that dream
of endless corridors, rooms within rooms,
mirrors on mirrors compulsively reflected;
while down the corridors, nearer and nearer,
came the great spiders delicately walking.

Courtesy

Do not throw a crumb lest the thrush
on your path should be suddenly flown,
taking away from you the round eye shining,
the softness and the freckles of feathers.

Do not speak even gently
lest the hill ponies, poised already
to gallop back to the crags, should leave you
hardly crediting that they came to your wall.

Gifts, gentling, were not asked
by these aliens, nor your love,
though you give it – and must then give
the courtesy of not showing love.

Focussing

In this photograph, each foreground leaf
is sharp – midrib and laterals
a miniature tree; enlarged enough
perhaps it would bear leaves, each with its tree.

Huge towers behind, unfocussed,
almost beyond perception,
loom vaguely, generalized,
subordinated by a "let's pretend",

a game not only pictures play
but days, their detail dwelt on
selectively, so that they seem
big with potential of other days the same.

Distanced but only half-ignored,
beyond the dear trivialities
the real subject looms, its shapes
huge, enigmatic, inescapable.

Burial Path

When we carried you, Siân, that winter day,
over four rivers and four mountains
to the burial place of your people,
it was not the dark rocks of Cwm-y-Benglog
dragged down my spirit,
it was not the steepness of Rhiw'r Ych
that cracked my heart.

Four by four, Siân, we carried you
over the mountain wilderness of Dewi,
fording Pysgotwr and Doithie,
crossing Camddwr by Soar-y-Mynydd,
Tywi at Nant-y-Neuadd; every river passed
brought us the challenge of another hill beyond.

Again and again from his rough pony's back, our leader
signalled with his hazel-staff of office
four, breathless, to lay down your coffin,
four, fresh in strength, to bear you
up the old sledge-ways, the sinew-straining tracks,
the steeps of Rhiw Gelynen and Rhiw'r Ych.

I with the rest, Siân, carried you.
The burial-path is long – forty times and more
I put my shoulder to the coffin
before the weary journey was accomplished
and down at last through leafless oaks
singing we carried you to the crumbling church,
the ancient yews, at the burial-place of your people.

It was not then my heart cracked, Siân,
nor my soul went into darkness.
Carrying you, there was great weariness,
and pride in an old ritual well performed –
our friend's firm leadership, smooth changes

from four to four, the coffin riding
effortlessly the surge of effort.
And at the grave, pride too in showing
churchmen how we of Soar knew well
ways of devotion, fit solemnity.

But with your grave whitened – the last ceremony –
and my neighbours, as I had urged them, gone ahead,
then it was I felt the weight of death
for the first time, Siân, and I knew
it would be always with me now
on the bitter journey that was not yet accomplished.

Now as I went down Rhiw'r Ych alone
and turned west over the ford of Nant-y-Neuadd,
I knew there was only darkness waiting
for me, beyond the crags of Cwm-y-Benglog.
It was then my heart cracked, Siân, my spirit
went into that darkness and was lost.

from *Not Without Homage* (1975)

At Strata Florida

This afternoon on the edge of autumn
our laughter feathers the quiet air
over tombs of princes. We idle
in an old nave, lightly approach
old altars. Our eyes, our hands
know fragments only; from these
the Abbey climbs and arches into the past.
We look up and find
only our own late August sky.

Ystrad Fflûr, your shadows fall
benevolently still on your ancient lands
and on us too, who touch your stones
not without homage. Take our laughter
on your consenting altars,
and to the centuries borne up
by your broken pillars, add
the light weight of an hour
at the end of summer.

Elegy for Sarah

Bitter apples load the tree
by a girl's grave
in a tangle of summer weeds.
Small wet apples glow
through summer rain.

"My days are past"
she cries from her stone,
"my purposes are broken off" –
apple bough broken,
fallen in dripping weeds.

"even the thoughts of my heart".
My thoughts, my purposes, my days
broken among weeds,
and summer rain falling
on wet stone, bitter apples.

Boy in a Train

Small boy, gently jolted along the suburban line,
horror-story spread on your bare knees,
your avid eyes have taken in the pictured beast,
black and alone on a storm-lit plain.

You look away now, out of the window, for reassurance,
at cluttered gardens, sheds and washing-lines.
You glance sideways at the woman slumped
in the next seat, her fat hands passive
on a draggled parcel. You are comforted,
your breath comes slower, you close the book
on that picture, wondering what you felt, and why.

No good, boy, no good. The beast of loneliness
looked at you too, and saw his host.
He has already started on his way
across the plain. Sooner or later,
whichever way you look for safety,
the black beast will be crawling in
at the corner of your eye.

Evening Wind

The hill wind tearing her white hair
reminded her of the sea.
Girls in button boots, she and her sisters
would run on the Capstan, laughing
at the scandalous evening wind
that swirled their great black skirts. Now
she walked faltering in an inland breeze
that stung her wrinkled face with salt
of breakers from seventy years ago.

Confrontation

There have been other such streets
hushed for the high-noon confrontation.
I know the smell of the dust, the feel
of scorching leather, the swish
of doors that for ever swing to.
I know how that small menacing shape,
black at the white street's end, will grow
to the wolf-lope, thin smile, poised
gun-hand of my unkillable foe.

Each time, my lucky shot leaves him
tumbled askew on the gasping street,
staring at the sun and smiling still,
as if he knew as well as I
that we have not yet trodden
the noon-white street where the story ends;
as if he knew as well as I
what the real end will be.

Stateless

In some nissen-hut of my mind
I have a stacked bed-roll, wooden chair,
suitcase plastered with peeling labels,
and a cheap clock measuring lethargic days.
I have no papers. Sometimes I am offered
forged ones, at too high a price.
Now you come, promising real
identity cards. Forgive me if till they arrive
I think it too early to rejoice.

Thirst

You say you love this rush-ridden valley
even in winter: even its ruins.
The love this land accepted once
was an instinctive one, not shaped in the brain,
not a sweetness in the heart, but acted only,
in the dumb tending of beasts and crops.

Now the land is offered your conscious devotion –
eulogized, courted, remembered, returned to.
Beware!
Something lives here that has an unquenchable thirst.
The bones of your life, drained dry of love,
would hardly be noticed in the rushes
of our insatiate valley.

Why?

Why, asked Leonardo,
why do the leaves
of the Star of Bethlehem
resemble the movement of water?
Seeing leaves flow, and ripples
crisping to leaf-shapes,
he asked not could there be a reason,
but what the reason was.
His jotted question was an act of faith.

Here in the intricate surface
of this uprooted oak
are correspondences, patterns,
astonishments. From every angle
it makes its point, achieves effects.
The play of light, straggle of fibre,
clinging of earth, give wood
a hundred textures, movements, new identities.
"Look!" I can say, but in my poverty
not formulate the living question
that in such ambiguity celebrates
eternally its answer.

Letter

Dear Sister, it seems to me long
since I waited last on you
in Summer at your house in Hereford
when we had Converse on manifold subjects
as of our Children and of matters
touching us both. It is much in my mind
today how I did then speak
of my dear Husband, saying
it was great Happiness to see
how having returned out of Hereford
to dwell in these Welsh Mountains
(the which are his Native Land),
he was no longer Sick nor burthened
in Spirit, but in New Health
and often merry, so that I too
could not forbear to laugh. Although
in very truth this Land of his
was never to my Mind nor Liking,
being far from towns
and much Afflicted with Great Rains and Floods,
and our Mansion House but a Poor Dwelling
with little comfort, by reason of its Age
and the Great Winds in these Hills.
But now my dear Sister it is long
since we spoke thus together
and had much Delight in converse
on these things, and in the Mild Airs
of that summer. For now all Tranquillity
has left me, since my dearest Husband
is Ill indeed, and of a strange Distemper,
so that we know not what Physic
may profit him, and can but pray
Almighty God to bring him safely through

this Fit of Sickness. And indeed, Dear Sister,
the Great Harshness of the Winter
amid these Rough Welsh Hills
and the long Hours of Darkness
(so that I am sometimes in Terror
that Light should not return, yet chide myself
greatly for such Folly, fit only for Children),
these things weigh heavy upon me
and would so more, but that I must
be always of good Heart in going
unto my Husband, that he may have no Fears.
So my dear Sister assure yourself always of my Love
and Thankfulness toward you, and pray to God
for us all, and that we may again
come to your House in time of Summer
as we did heretofore. Your humble Servant
and truly loving Sister, Jane Vaughan.

Sheep in the Hedge

This is no mild and never-never sheep,
but a heavy wild thing, mad with fright,
catapulting at you from a noose of brambles,
hurtling back into worse frenzy of tangles.
Don't imagine you are welcome.
Don't expect gratitude.
That woolly maniac would hate you
if she had any consciousness to spare
from panic. She can see sideways.
There is too much world forcing itself
through slit eyes into her dim brain –
a spiky overpowering pattern of thorns.
Now, worst of all, she suffers the sight of you
(no doubt malevolent) hideously near,
touching her! She wrenches, rips, breaks out,
knocks you into the hedge and is away,
her plump bedraggled body jogging down the road
full-pelt on sticks of legs, pert hooves. You are left
to mop your dripping scratches and stitch up
the tatters of your good intentions.

Hanging Days

Plenty were sorry to see them go,
the shows by Tarell bridge.
Brecon would be full as a skin
on a hanging day –
good for trade, good for the soul.

Thousands would come and wait on the river bank
and on the bridge, staring up
at the gallows under the prison wall.
There was always a sigh when they led him out
to stand under the noose. Every time
something fresh to enjoy, to teach your children –
we have lost a lot, with the old pleasures gone.

There was so much in a hanging, after all –
a warning, and a drama; you could hate
that fellow there – cheat, robber,
murderer, even, on a lucky day –
and pity him too, love him almost.
Choking death would take him today
and stay away from you, perhaps, for that much longer.

And they, of course, the doomed ones,
were in their glory. How they rose
to the occasion! – made improving speeches
to the crowd, forgave the hangman
and everyone for miles! One sang
heart-rending hymns and got us all to join
in harmony: another led in prayer
for half an hour or more – the chaplain
(a new lad, pale already) was quite outfaced.

And the hard ones, decked for death
in delicate finery, or scorning him with their rags –
they gave some splendid moments,
forgiving nobody, refusing clergy,
laughing in the gentry's faces – you could smell brimstone!

Myself, it was the girls I would go miles for.
One her prying neighbour found
forcing her baby's corpse into a peat-pool.
Seventeen she was, all eyes in a thin white face.
We had the biggest crowd for months
to see her die. She showed no shame
and would not pray – just gave us back our stares
till she was hooded, noosed, and jerked
into blackness. Who would have missed
such a sinner, such a memory!

Yes, we have lost a lot these days.
It was good to see a death we thought deserved –
our eyes used up that death; for a little while
we felt safe. We were proved wrong
time and again, but still came back
to win our space of peace out of that
permitted violence, now hidden
dirtily in a furtive cell. Death is the same
as ever. It is we who have lost the knack
of looking at him, now that when we meet
we are never sure he is deserved.

Carn Cafall

Arthur's great hound Cafall,
nosing and lolloping through the hills
over against Rhaeadr
on the track of the swine Troynt,
printed a stone for ever with his paw.
His warrior master built a cairn,
crowned with the stone message
set there to wait – how many centuries? –
high on Carn Cafall in Buellt –
a cryptogram crying for its decipherer.
He who had come to his kingdom
through a stone that to him alone
gave up the sword it gripped,
honoured this other stone, knew Cafall
had been the pen and not the writer,
and reverenced a sign
ordained, though dark to him then.

Many took the stone
in after years, kept it the space
of a day and a night, stared wondering
at the great pawmark. Some knew themselves
ignorant, baffled – were not surprised
to find it gone, when they woke
from a twitching sleep, back to its rough home
to wait another year or century.
Some thought they saw lines of meaning,
felt a drumming in the brain, slept unwillingly
as though drugged, struggling not to slacken
hold on the stone. They woke with empty hands,
feeling a wind as if of the mountain
sweep from their minds the memory
of yesterday's half-understanding.

The cairn is unvisited now, the hill-name garbled
on maps that forget the paths
where the king's hounds drove red-eyed Troynt,
ravager of fields, destroyer of towns
(with wrath, Glyn Gothi sang, with wounds and violence) –
Troynt, lusting to plunge his tusks at the root of towers.
Arthur sleeps, with Cafall at his feet.
Through another winter, and another,
the enigmatic stone endures unread
the assault of storm. Troynt, his gashes healed,
snuffles and stirs, and only half-asleep
scents the old swine-paths over waiting hills.

Seven Found Poems

(from 17th- and 18th-century Mss in Shrewsbury Archives)

1. Blandishment

Could thanks admit
of the swiftness of thoughts,
gratitude had ere this
rode post to salute you.

(Dorothy Phillips to her aunt Alice Lloyd, 9 Aug., 1650).

2. Advice

My desire is, that such a temper
may be found for the matter among yourselves
before the child be sent for
that nothing may seem to be done
by way of difference and contention.

Nature though in some cases
it must submit to law, is enough to make
such a submission uneasy
and a kind of state of violence to us.

Try therefore, good Madam,
what the fair obliging way will do –
most pleasing to God,
most easy to yourselves,
and most to the child's benefit.

(Henry Price to Frances Eyton, 18 May, 1704).

3. Solicitude

Pray make much of yourself
and take less care upon you
towards your old age.
Being so great a stranger
to that slavery in your youth,
they that are in their grave
would have wondered you should have made
so great a slave of yourself.
God content you! and I should be glad
you lessened your troubles
for your health's sake.

(Elizabeth Lochard to her sister Frances, early 18th century).

4. The Law

(a)
Madam, I have sent the deeds.
Let the little deed
be executed first;
and if you have any money, pay it him,
and let him put it up before the witnesses,
and when the witnesses are gone
you may take it again.

(Arthur Hanmer to Frances Eyton, 16 March 1693/4).

(b)
I have no news to send you,
having no leisure in the day
to take any diversion,
but am daily plagued
and tormented by scoundrelly fellows,
and am glad when the evening comes
when I go to the Devil for relief,
where I meet young lawyers.

(Thomas Hanmer to Rice Hanmer, 5 Sept. 1721).

5. Resolution

Rather than lie under so heavy a cloud
as is coming upon me,
I must put at stake
all my wife's interest in North Wales.
For to what purpose should I hazard all here
for a long expectation there? And in fine
it is not Sir Richard Mason's riches
nor greatness shall cast me down,
though it happens in an ill crisis
of time, but however I'll not leave
a stone unturned but I will retrieve
that which in right of my wife is justly due
to, honoured Madam, your most affectionate
and most obliged servant.

(William Probert to Dorothy Hanmer, 24 Feb. 1671/2).

6. Herbal

Alecost, mountain thyme,
Borage, ground ivy,
Cardus, lavender tops,
Alexander, betony, balm,
Mint, saladin, clare,
Fennel, sweetfern, sage red,
Pillotar of the Wall,
Angilliere, wormwood,
Dragones, scabious, rue,
Rosemary, mugwort,
Pimpernel that grows in the Corn,
Tormentil, egramony, roseafolis,
Storoiam, coslops.

(List by Frances Eyton, undated).

7. Grievance

Dear mother, I wonder at you,
and take it very unkind
that you are so urgent at me
to lay out money for Sidney.
I will not lay out any more money
for them nor nobody else.
Dear mother, consider, I am but a servant
and have nothing but what I work hard for:
therefore I desire you would stop your hand:
and solicit no more for nobody,
but consider how young you sent me out
above all the rest, and what hardship I had
to come up on my feet, and yet
I have been a mother and a slave to them all
instead of a sister, and have laid out money –
a crown? Nay, I may say pounds
and not less, and now I think it is time
to shut up and look at home
except I get more thanks for my pains.
I am sure I have had a great care
and taken great pains
to get what I have, and go to my bed
with many an aching heart and bone
and tired limb that you know nothing of,
but you all think that I get money
very easily, and let me undergo
what hardship I will. Methinks you might
have employed your pen in something else
than soliciting for Sidney: in
congratulating me or joining me in prayers
for my safe delivery out of a great rogue's hand
who designed to have ruined and made a beggar of me –
for when he found another man
came into my company, so that he could not
have his desire, then he raised

all the scandalous reports he could
to take away my good name.
That is all one, I see very plain
out of sight and out of mind,
only so far as serves everybody's turn,
no matter what becomes of me,
sink or swim.

(Alice Owen to her parents, 20 May 1712).

Witness

Talking to his grown-up visiting daughter
opposite me in the train,
he uses me as audience,
half-turns to include me.
She courteously tolerates his questions,
enriches niggardly answers
with a smile. To believe in a bond
with this cool stranger he must have my
complicity. He chatters, covering
uncertainty, invokes minutiae
of a shared past. I am to witness
that they are as close as ever – she
knows they are not. He laughs often,
but his eyes call
"My daughter, my daughter",
after a ghost that dwindles
down-wind.

Trust

In grey marches of sky and valley-rim
a hawk screams; an alien life claws mine,
then lets go.

A squirrel, rippling upward, pauses. Eyes
involve me briefly in total otherness,
then I am alone.

In a look, in a cry, beings complete without me
own me for a tyranny of seconds,
then are gone.

Slowly and late I learn how trust can sing
after the bird-cry fades, and how it shines
from the empty tree.

Supper

With evening came rain,
and with darkness a dark sound
in the bending trees.
I did not draw the curtains
for supper. In the black panes
our copies sat at table, and like us
turned each to other, smiling.
Light picked out fair hair,
a lifted glass. But in that room,
whose walls were superimposed on night
too thinly to hide the patterns of rain,
shadows were absolute, one
with sensed unseen mountains
beyond us to the north.
We ate well, laughed, were warm,
sheltered; but not at ease.
Each time the black window drew our eyes
we saw a known room strange
and unstable with storm, saw too
those threatened selves who had let such darkness in.

Messenger

Is there a formula for telling bees
of a stranger's death? They are remote
in the wild upper garden, yet however aloof
and preoccupied, they require to know
of crisis and celebration. They take offence
at a breach of their code, may suffer
a psychosomatic sickness,
swarm inaccessibly, or leave en masse.

The bees do not know me. Today
there is no-one skilled in their wishes
who has time for them; death came unforeseen
to an old man resting here, and broke the calm
of the ordered house. I have no
ritual phrases for this occasion,
but am the only messenger
available. How should I speak to them?

Perhaps they will not expect ceremony
from one who is no concern of theirs.
Perhaps it is permissible to approach,
making as little stir as possible,
through the huge hemlock and old black-currant bushes,
and stooping at each white-slatted house
say only, "Bees, an old man has died –
I do not know his name".

Tourists

Warner, setting out eagerly from Bath
at five on a lively morning
for the inspiring rigours of Wales
with obliging C------, equipped himself for adventure
with a rusty but respectable spencer
(good enough for North Wales, he said).
The travellers' huge pockets bulged with clothes,
maps, and little comforts; their heads were full
of Ossian, whose horrendous glooms
they were gratified to recognise
one evening on the road to Rhaeadr
(though Ossian had not prepared them
for the state of the road, or the shortage
of bedchambers at the 'Lion').
Romantic tourists, no doubt, perpetual
outsiders, but willing to love,
and finding much "singular, striking
and indescribable". They were comic
(embarrassed at being spotted,
with their pedlars' pockets, by fashionable females),
but worked hard for their exaltations,
plodding twenty-five miles to Machynlleth
north over boggy mountains, or stumbling
two hours across rocks to find a guide
to Dôlbadarn ruins. They were uncomplaining
on Snowdon in a thick mist (they drank milk
gratefully, but longed for brandy), and did not grumble
when, at Aberglaslyn, salmon failed to leap
(only two would even try). Who can say
that at the end of August, leaving Chepstow
for flood-tide at the ferry, they were taking
nothing real away, or that their naïve and scholarly wonder
had given nothing in return?

Dragon

West wind sets the dragon rippling over the flag,
launches a legend to whip its scaly tail
out through the trees, pad through Rhyd Goch
(splashes slithering off metallic flanks)
and pace Cefn Fanog at dusk, be glimpsed
as a dark sinuosity on the hill,
a distant puff of red-lit smoke.

Is it kin to the dragon, cast as villain,
that slants an unjudging eye upon
its unvindictive slayer, and coils
in elegant agony round the saint's
transfixing lance? Or are all dragons one
with the winged and convoluted image of life?
This perhaps is a maverick among dragons,
ill at ease in such portentous company.

West wind dies before dark tonight.
Last of light finds the flag hardly fluttered,
dragon hidden in folds. Whatever went plashing
through the ford, whatever slid along
the darkening hill, now rests again,
but is a light sleeper. That image it leaves
of antique and raffish splendour
is vigorous, if unclear; and likely to recur.

from *The Print of Miracle* (1978)

Hoofprints

The legend was always here,
at first invisible, poised above the hill,
stiller than any kestrel. Idle hands
carved hoofprints on a rock
by the hill path. The legend, venturing nearer,
breathed warm as blessing. At last
men recognized it. A magic horse
had leapt from hill to hill, they said,
the day the valley began. Could they not see
his prints, that had waited in the rock
till guided hands revealed them?
From the unseeable, legends leap.
In the rock of our days
is hidden the print of miracle.

Arthur

No grave, no grave for Arthur.
Beyond Camelot's rootless towers
is a truth sharing the nature of rock –
hard, grey, pock-marked, lasting:
and sharing the nature of fire –
a gleam in wilderness, a sword against ice:
and sharing the nature of food –
simple and subtle, a need, a delight.
Badon is bread, bread put into our hands.

All Souls'

Shutting my gate, I walk away
from the small glow of my banked fire
into a black All Souls'. Presently
the sky slides back across the void
like a grey film. Then the hedges
are present, and the trees, which my mind
already knows, are no longer
strangers to my eyes.
The road curves. Further along,
a conversation of lights begins
from a few houses, invisible except as light,
calling to farms that higher in darkness
answer still, though each now speaks
for others that lie dumb.
Light at Tŷmawr above me, muted by trees,
is all the voice Brongwesyn has,
that once called clearly enough
into the upper valley's night.
From the hill Clyn ahead
Glangwesyn's lively shout of light
celebrates old Nant Henfron, will not let
Cenfaes and Blaennant be voiceless.
I am a latecomer, but offer
speech to the nameless, those
who are hardly a memory, those
whose words were always faint
against the deafening darkness
of remotest hills.
For them tonight when I go home
I will draw back my curtains, for them
my house shall sing with light.

Clehonger Thorn

Woman, I tell you it was blood that ran,
not sap – my axe drew blood!
I'll not touch that thing again,
that devil's thorn, or God's –
let it grow, let it spawn
its pale wrong-season flowers
and draw the gang of gapers here
on each Old Christmas Eve!

Let all the miracle-chasing louts
in Herefordshire come here
trampling my land with lumpish boots
in January night – some huffing in
just before twelve, their breath in their hands!

Blood is nothing when it spouts
from a slaughtered beast, or even
from a man's wound – the one you let flow,
the other you staunch. But what do you do
when a tree bleeds, but pray?

At Nevern

Nevern, signed with David's cross and Brynach's,
lay hushed and innocent. We stood
in the sunny churchyard. Tower and trees
rippled with heat-haze, as if a tiny breeze
passed over baptismal water
in a golden font. On Carn Ingli above,
Brynach walked with angels; the afternoon
was a pause in their conversation.
Silence surrounded the laughter of children
who broke from yew-trees' shadow
to run between the tombs.
Perception reached out to the hills
tentatively as a hand
to a loved face. Unborn words
were given into winged keeping.
In dusk on the northward road
we were too far away to hear
when at the carn the voices began again.

Acquaintance

It was from a border county of my life
you crossed into another country,
having never settled. Smoke rose one dawn
from the overnight house for which
your thrown stone transitorily defined
a patch of my waste land; but soon
the hut was derelict. Acquaintance ending
seems not to warrant uneasier weather
than a fraction of wind-change brings;
yet over my moors the sky sags now,
black with irrational certainty
of departures. From your hasty thatch
rushes loosen, blow east. The heartland may be next
to know depopulation.

Drinking Stone

You offer me your stories
laughing, to show I may laugh, to say
you are sure I must mock
at such old childishness.
Tonight by your fire I listen
to tales of the drinking stone
that each midsummer cockcrow
goes thirsty down to the stream.
I am not to think you credit
that shuddering heave of stone
from the suck of earth, that gliding
over still-dark fields, that long drinking.
You tell it laughing, wary of my response,
but I shall not think you credulous.
It is I who thirstily drink
wonders, I who from dawn mist mould
a grey shape, sated, going home.

Gwlad Yr Hâf

"Oh, I could almost reach across!" she would say.
It was so close, my mother's country,
but I would not own it. To see it clearly
meant rain. I stared resentfully
over narrow but unmistakable sea
at those other hills, and refused
to acknowledge kinship. She would coax me
to the window, trying to show me
fields over Minehead way – it was true,
one could see green on those too-clear slopes
in the doomed sunlight. It pained her that I
so rarely wanted to look. I could not speak
of my own nature's alienated lands,
my need to have one coast only, my fear
of the dark weather already drumming
through the straits of my blood.

Iconoclast

"Take down the Sun and Moon", he ordered,
shutting behind him the day's last church door.
His mare, tethered, turned on him
her simple gaze devoid of censure,
which he was free to think a welcome.
That night he wrote, soberly exultant,
"Today we broke down sixty superstitious Pictures,
some Popes and Crucifixes, and God the Father
sitting in a Chair, and holding a Glass in his Hand".

Listing them on the smug page, he frowned to find
images unbroken in his mind's tabernacle –
"three of God the Father,
and three of Christ and the Holy Lamb,
and three of the Holy Ghost
like a Dove with Wings;
and the Twelve Apostles carved
in Wood on the Top of the Roof,
and Two Mighty Great Angels with Wings".

Sleep dragged him down to suffer
the trumpeted charge of carven cherubim.
Battered by a thousand wooden wings, he lay
broken, listening in terror, understanding nothing,
while the great Angels he had left for dead
still cried aloud God's message
in the forbidden language of beauty.

Standing Stone

The stone stands among new firs,
still overtoppping them. Soon
they will hide it. Their lower branches
will find its cold bulk
blocking their growth. After years,
lopped trunks will lie piled,
awaiting haulage. The stone will stand
in a cleared valley, and offer again
the ancient orientation.

The stone stores, transmits.
Against its almost-smoothness
I press my palms. I cannot ask,
having no word of power,
no question formed. Have I
anything to give? My hands offer
a dumb love, a hope towards
the day of the freed valley.
Flesh fits itself to the slow curve
of dominating stone, as prayer
takes the shape of a god's will.

A mindless ritual is not empty.
When the dark mind fails, faith lives
in the supplication of hands
on prayer-wheel, rosary, stone.
It is evening. I walk down-valley
on an old track. Behind me
the ephemeral trees darken.
Among them, the stone waits.

Guest

She strains the fragile evening,
stretching it too far.
Tomorrow's butts and dregs
will be comment enough;
forbearance becomes you.
Her coat, drooping from a chair,
fails to catch her eye;
she is deaf to the broken-backed crash
of the last grey log.
But now, as the garden shivers
in a night-wind from the hills,
she cannot escape grim chatter of leaves
on dark panes, or longer pretend
that the evening is still alive.
Your gentleness, patient with slow goodbyes,
protects her from discomfiture. At last
under her car's rakish pressure
the cattle-grid shakily shouts;
from the encompassment of your window's lights
she is gone. She sees them once,
through rain, at the turn of the road.
All the way home, they shelter her still.

Film, Aran Islands

In this film of an island from the air
walls make a pattern like leafless ivy-stems,
the island the stone they grip –
stems without hope of growth,
tightly in death resisting
prisings of time and weather.

Man's life rooted, spread, gripped
on this hard island till sap dried.
The walls he left go on
uselessly resisting the salty wind.

The camera tricks us into truth
with its image of a tenacity
reason finds barren, and the heart
coaxes into a yield of small dark berries.

Colour-slide

I have been sorting slides all day.
What do I remember, this winter evening?
Ten-year-old snow froths up
through a June lake; castles drown in corn.
Child's face and man's, imperfectly echoing
each other, alike chiefly
in vulnerability, surface in turn.
Streets run down to a beach,
all beaches, where selves by the score
laze in a composite summer.
A church, a sorrel-patch, dead friends,
blue ice and a lorry-load of rhubarb
are tossed up and sink back
into the cauldron. One picture
I salvage intact – a lit shed
full of white turkeys fattening,
with three months to live. They are caught
in the everlasting limbo of my slide,
row towering behind row, pink necks craned
and dot-eyed heads all turned
to the encapsulating click. Why have I isolated
this picture from the brew? Perhaps
it is because these creatures' days
were more obviously numbered, and because for them
merciful callousness spares me
too sharp concern. While all I might weep for
in the boxed past is now obscured
in a bubbling of images, these funny birds are clear,
staring, silently gobbling "Gone, gone, gone!"

May

Here-and-gone shadows in the river
are small trout. Sharp flint,
cutting dark across ripples,
is shadow of a bird.
Hawthorn, tilted
by last winter's gales,
leans like a willow,
yields as a sacrifice
the image of its flowers
for blurring by water,
shaking by trout-shadows,
wounding by dark flint.

The language of vulnerable sun
has one word only
for love, give, ask, be,
and in a million evanescent shapes
utters it like a prayer.

Carved Capital

Hands divined the forms
trapped in the stone tree, and gave
the permitted cuts that freed them.
They oozed out, squamous, pot-bellied,
beaked, muzzled, footed, clawed,
and took up their grotesque eternal pose.

One, man-shaped, too slow escaping,
caught by the sculptor's down-tools moment,
stayed half-pillar for ever,
stretching a splayed hand roofwards,
blank hands and twisted mouth
an agonized and lasting comment.

At his locked feet a little rabbit,
eyes bulging and ears down,
joined the shape of its perpetual fear
to the grotesquerie, frustration, pain,
that high on a tree in the stone forest
bodied again the pattern of celebration.

Red

Small and still, the hedgehog crouched
in the shining road. He had accomplished
little of that sluggish perilous crossing.
His prickly-proofed coat had availed him nothing.
In five miles of autumn from hamlet to village
his was the finest red, soft berries of blood
springing from nostrils and little jaws.
He was still warm. He would harden soon
in that meek posture, with two paws
at his face, as if helping death
to darken his eyes. Quiet and blind
he crouched in the sun. Exultant there sang
for a while, till it darkened and dulled,
loud as October leaves, the splendid red.

Burial Cist

Drought had shrivelled the bogs
on the high moor. Peat dried
uncut, unstacked. A hardness
struck up through yellow grass.
Searching for an ancient grave
we scattered, quartering arid acres, peering
into powdery base of tussocks, seeking signs.
Thunder lurked in the huge sky.

From long dykes braced with leaning stones
we sighted the distant fire-hill
across a hidden valley, and called,
launching our small shouts through hot haze,
each hailing another's dark archetypal shape
on the moving skyline. One waved, pointed, ran.
We converged on a broken mound, hardly higher now
than the rough clumps around it.

By the little slab-lined grave,
open and empty, we were silent.
Below the moor the crags, below the crags the road
and the coming rains waited, and the coming days.
Now in our tiredness we were undiversified,
human only, sunk in the primeval crouch.

Pwll Yr Afallen

"Come to the apple pool!" she called,
running down to its green deeps.
But when she paused on the petalled shore
he was gone, hidden again
among brittle branches of laughter
on the dry hill. Slowly she stepped
alone into the water, and took its coldness
into her silence.
           In the arid lightness
of barren trees he awaited
her sure return. A small wind off the pool
put its arms round him, unrebuffed,
momentarily bringing the moist scent
of an apple-blossom shore.

Cats Dancing

Autumn evening. The builders had gone home,
rattling away down the stony track.
Their scaffolding imposed its arbitrary frames
on rectangles of darkening sky,
darker trees and hills.
                                        Coming tired
from the kitchen's brightness and clatter
to sharp air in the porch, I caught
a movement, a ripple of dark on dark,
and opening the door wider could then see
three black-and-gold cats, young, wild,
hungry, yet seeming to care for nothing
but their own elegant, unpredictable
subtleties of movement.
                                        In their grace
the evening danced, pivoting
on the lighted house in its metal frame.
Steel and stone were one
with the rising house of winter, in the dancing moment.

At the slam of a door, the cats were gone.
Time was sequence again, the trees
stood back darkly. Night drew on.

Safaddan

(Many stories are told of Llyn Safaddan – Llangorse Lake – in Breconshire. The River Llyfni, which flows through it, is said never to mingle its waters with those of the lake. There are tales of a city buried under the lake. The birds of Safaddan sing only for the rightful heir to the throne of Wales. Giraldus says that three knights once put this tradition to the test. The two Anglo-Normans got no response to their commands, but for Gruffydd ap Rhys ap Tewdwr every bird cried aloud and beat its wings.)

Through bruised reeds my boat thrust
into open water. First light broke thin mist
and was broken in a scatter of brightness
on the grey lake. In the depths
Llyfni coursed, eternally separate,
spurning the lake-waters beyond
intangible banks of its own force.
Silent lay the drowned city of legend
with its aqueous colonnades.

I had never seen the lake so thronged with birds
or known them so quiet. Hundreds there were,
out on the water, on the island,
and secret among the reeds.
On the further shore, three horsemen
rode to the lake's edge. Two dismounted,
each in turn shouting over the water –
I could not hear the words. From all
that intricate pattern of stilled wings
and watchful eyes, not one bird startled up.
The shouting sank dully into the lake.

Now the third rider, tall on a tall white horse,
slowly paced down to the hushing waters,
dismounted, knelt in prayer. I shipped my oars
and was quiet as the birds. When he stood
in the growing sunlight, knowledge came to me.
I knelt in the boat. He called.
All round me, suddenly, were wings
beating the water, rustling the reeds,
and a thousand songs of homage rose.
My boat rocked on the joyful surge
of Llyfni's invisible stream, my ears
were dazed with triumphant proclamations
of sunken bells, and louder and louder
the All Hails of Safaddan's birds.
Lake and kingly rider and host of birds,
and I with them, were caught up into the sun.

Fragmented sun on sliding water:
reed-beds thick at the lake's verge:
the island low astern. Three distant riders
dwindling on a path away from the shore.
Tired, I reached for the oars.
I had never seen so many birds
on the lake. They were lifting, one by one
or dense in wedge-shaped flights.
It was quiet. There was only
my oars' creak-and-plash
and the soft rush of departing wings.

Lighting Candles

Tonight, after storm, lighting candles,
I remember a picture I have seen
of Indian women at night
launching candles on leaf-boats
to float away downstream,
carrying prayers into the dark.

Tonight, lighting candles, I think
of the dark faces, the dwindling lights,
night closing back, the water
black again, reflections gone,
boats all sailed away, and the prayers
now rising from some further reach
of the sacred river. Out of sight
the dancing end of the little flames.

Tonight I light candles.
What prayers were waiting
for these new bodies of fire?
Standing outside, I see
upon a dark and turbulent sky
my house launched, with a freight of light.

from *Lighting Candles* (1982)
(new poems section)

Blizzard

"What is it like up here in snow?"
we wondered, shivering at dusk
on the boggy plateau. Answerless,
we stared along the ruts
of an obscure track. There was
the hint of a wind. Our thoughts
momentarily touched a sleeping fear.

That fear has woken up tonight
with a white scream. Even the valley
suffers the storm's answer
that we so lightly sought –
the truth from the heights
come shrieking down in darkness
to batter at our safety.

In the morning, when the wind drops,
we will climb again, perhaps,
and in the high white silence find
another answer growing from the first.
Because that was, this is – sun, sun and snow,
and all tracks gone but those
our seeking footsteps make upon the hill.

Heol y Mwyn (Mine Road)

Butting the wet wind, we stumbled
along Heol y Mwyn. The sky
trawled for us with nets of drizzle
grey as the lead mined once
in the wilderness upstream.
Soaked, blinded, we crouched for refuge
in an old adit.
                            "Listen!" you said.
Now we could hear not only
the shush of rain over the shaggy surface
of the hill, but somewhere far within it
the hollow fall of water into water,
the unceasing enigmatic speech
of depth and darkness.
                            The wind veered,
the sky drew in its nets, empty.
Freely we walked up a sunny valley.
Our lightest words had now
more gentleness, since we had known,
together, the chill uneasy sound
of the hill's hidden waters, falling,
falling, for ever into dark.

A Slight Stroke

For years there had come to him,
always unpredictably,
the sense of morning on bare hills –
sun, great stones, larks rising –
a promise spelt obscurely
in the land's lines, and answered
by silent amens of the heart.

Those years ended; when,
he could not say – with youth perhaps,
or at the clouding-over of love,
or in the heavy plodding
along a digressive track,
after some unremembered
misreading of the compass.

Now his death had touched him
for the first time, brushing face,
arm, thigh, with gentle fingers,
promising return.
He felt within himself the cold
of great stones black on a bare hill
after moonlight, before dawn.

He knew this land. He rested
in its chill dusk, and waited
for the first springing-up
and the remembered song
of larks, with sunlight on their wings.

Girls Laughing

I can remember laughing like that.
Two girls, folding a sheet
down there in the sun,
stagger with laughter, willingly lose
to a snatching breeze, to breathlessness,
to bulging unstable exuberance
stretched between them.
Sheet-corners escape, flap snapping.
Tugged off-balance by swell and jerk
of uncontrollable life,
two girls, weeping, laugh and laugh.

Stop

(Abíshiktananda writes that no beauty ever stops the monk,
"for he knows something more beautiful than all beauty").

What is it like to be
never stopped by beauty,
knowing something more beautiful?

By the altar, slate tablets
darkly enrich the wall,
carved script curling to celebrate
the obscure.
             Outside
on a sunny tombstone,
a fat green caterpillar promenades,
shiny black head like a pinching shoe
at the end of a bulging leg.

Laboriously, the earth turns.
The caterpillar goes home
into hogweed and scabious.
Sunlight moves eastward up the nave,
stroking dim names.
Richard, Harriet, Huw,
have you answers now?

My hand follows the flow
of lettering, slides over slate,
savours the rasping ruggedness
of the wall.
             Such love
out of its very disproportion
breeds, minuscule as lichen, trust,
nurtured by this old silent place.

I go out into low sunlight,
content to be dazzled, momentarily
knowing no stop, momentarily
seeing in that bright blindness,
plain to read as a child's alphabet,
the hieroglyphs of beauty.

Gone Out

They have gone out.
The old house and the new
are silent. Indifferent sheepdogs
bark perfunctorily, back away
to muddy recesses of the yard
or slink through broken doors
into the dusk of barns.

On the hill-brow is reared
the new house, empty as yet.
Its white eyes look south
across the river. Garden, trees,
the litter of life, are still to come,
in years that spread before it
like the huge plain and skyline mountains.

The old house, not derelict yet,
stands on the yard.
On flaking steps to the tall porch
are tubs of flowers, their petals
riffled by a breeze that speaks
long and obscurely in shade-sycamores.
Windows reaching from ground
to shabby eaves accept
the farmyard with its fringe
of blue sacks, yellow tins,
its bulk of malthouse and granary,
the boast of Richard Price who built this Pile –
strong lines of wealth achieved and burgeoning.

Only the idle dogs are here
in flesh, warm, muddy-coated.
Everyone has gone out.

Journeys

I have forgotten stations we stopped at,
how old I was, how long the journey,
who sat opposite, how bags were stowed,
which wind-groomed White Horse
we galloped past, everything
but the rattling race of the train
through landscapes of anticipation,
and, now, one scene – a hillside meadow
below woods, a grey house
at the edge of trees.

This was the destination
I at once wanted, hung out
into ear-aching wind to hanker after,
was hurried far away from,
forgot for years.
                    From what stop
on what journey comes the memory
of arrival at dusk, candle to bed,
(I a child in the loved house)?
Woken by sound that swelled
from dream to day, I ran
to the deepset window, watched
below the meadow blue with harebells
the train pass by, and waved to a child
who leaned out, longingly it seemed,
smaller and smaller, gone in a moment.
I turned then, ran downstairs, forgot.

Warm Day

This is the year's first warmth,
fragile yet, harried by a shrewd wind.
A yellow bulldozer, high on a new farm-road,
adds another line to the hill.
The roar of its brown churning
fills the valley. Wind slackens
and the sound fails, drops to a secretive mutter
behind the sharp calling of lambs.

Here in the churchyard
three children idle, on their way anywhere,
scuffing shoes on grass-grown tiles
of what was once a nave.
Across the fields, a hopeful pony whinnies.
Suddenly purposeful, the children are gone.
Grass on grave-mounds sifts and sifts
all that is left of the wind.

The far-off bulldozer grinds on
along Rhiw Garreg Lwyd, cutting across
the monks' road, the sheep-paths and the drovers' tracks.
This year, lorries will carry lime to the high slopes.
Long-abandoned hill will be re-seeded.

The children and the pony
have found each other.

Air nuzzles the yew-trees.
The day's warmth strengthens.
Its only promise – of summer – seems enough.

Defences

Here and there everywhere
at all hours
are battenings-down,
nailings-up, buttressings,
reinforcings. Here,
chain-saws sound from the forest;
across the fields
far-off tapping starts again –
fence-post, stockade. Claps
of blasting from quarries
splinter miles of air. Clinking
sharp-soft as bird-call
may be distant heaping
of stone on stone.
Those old walls on the hill,
growing once more from grass,
are one row higher each dawn.
There were lights up there
again last night.
                           Hope
chooses its omens; the heron heads
for better weather,
upstream or down.
Hold your breath. Hear
the patching of the world:
the shoring-up of burrows,
the grasses digging in.

from *Kindred* (1986)

Kindred

I am still a mile or two
from the source. In spite of myself
I hear the stony flow of the stream
as speech, though not about anything
I know. No bleating, no bird-call;
the only other sound is a breeze
over molinia-grass. It is hard
not to think of a sigh.

On either hand the shallow slope
of the bank steepens, further up,
to a low hill; behind that
rises high land. Nothing seems to grow
for miles but long pale grass
in ankle-turning clumps. My mind
sees little horns of moss on the moors,
cups of lichen on grey rocks,
red-green of whinberry leaves.

Round the next curve of the stream
low broken walls delineate a life
almost beyond my imagining.
Something calls, with a voice
seeming at first as alien
as the stream's, yet inescapable,
and after a while more like
the calling of kindred,
or my own voice echoing
from a far-off encompassing wall.

Last Words

They came for his last counsel,
saying "Tell us now, tell us,
sum your life for us before you go.
We need the right question,
the sufficient answer."

He turned his head stiffly on the pillow,
and muttered of a curving wall
and moss on stone, of wind in the hedge
by the top gate, the stir and trample
of uneasy mares. He whispered
of a russet hill across the river,
and on the bank one golden tree.

"It is too late," they said,
"he is babbling." They touched his hand,
and went away.

He felt the resistance of stone,
the fragile antennae of moss
and its plushy deeps. He heard
a breeze in the hazel, and soft snorting
of gentled mares. At the river,
whirl upon whirl rose over him
the golden leaves, a visual song,
balance of phrase and phrase,
question and answer.

Banquet

(At the time of the 19th-century religious revivals it was said of two old North Breconshire women, "The Revival was a banquet for them.")

Their youth was poor and barren as the land.
The mould that should have formed them women
held some flaw, broke early,
spilling them out to harden into things
men's eyes would never rest on
except with scorn.
                      They were strong, though.
Fighting their stony patch
on its shelf of rock, they won.
The mound-encircled garden was rough, plain,
growing food, not flowers; yet as they touched
the juicy crispness of new sap-filled leaves
they learned a kind of tenderness.

By rushlight at the dark of the year,
when knitting-pins made winter music,
they could remember those great skies
spread lordly-wise above them when they wandered
hill-pastures, scratting grey tough wool
from fence and thorn.
                      Year after year
came back thaw, singing, airy softness,
pulsing of the blood, to tease and mock,
then gale and fall of leaf and snow
to tell them what they knew too well.

Then, when they were almost old, he came.
He preached in the river-meadow
to crowds who wept and begged and leapt,

cried "Glory, glory!", fell
foaming on the rough tussocks of grass.
He seemed to speak softly, yet from the hill
they heard, and from their hut came
fearfully, like unhandled ponies.
He looked up, smiled. They were unused to love.
This thing seemed other than the rut and musk
most knew (not they). Stumbling,
each clutching the other on the sliding stones,
they took the short cut down.

That was the start of it – their banqueting-time,
wine of God, and gold, and bath
of sweetest milk, damask tent
and bed of silk, lemon-grove,
low-hung moon, summer, subtle song,
their rest, their dawn, their piercing love.

The dark time came again. They rattled logs
into flame, and shadows walked the wall.
They grew old, hunched over the hearth.
One muttered words he taught,
the other joined her in her prayer,
catching at the rags of a memory. Snow
sifted under the door. Each stretched her hands
to the fire, like a beggar,
and waited for the placing in her palm
of a small dole of love.

Cat and Skull

Here is the skull of a young ram,
small slightly-curving horns
longer than they would seem
if springing from curly wool.
Perched on a tree-stump chopping-block,
its empty-socketed, broken-nosed face
is turned to stream and hills.
Tiny busy creatures scurry
into and from its cavities.

Towards it saunters the golden-eyed cat
in her pride of fur, her splendour
of marmalade, tabby and white.
Her head tilts, her paw is up to pat
at the grey-white, meatless remembrancer.
She topples it, casually, feeling no need
for confrontation. In the spread-whiskered,
plump contentment of her here and now
she pads on, not hungry, but always reserving
the right to kill. The skull
lies upside down in the grass.
Sun warms it a little, as it does
tree-stump and grass and the cat's fur.

Edward Bache advises his Sister

(A found poem from a letter of 1802, written from Ludlow.)

Dear Sister,
Although I have no reason
to suspect you of misconduct,
yet my affection and solicitude
will, I hope, excuse these lines
of brotherly advice.
Being visited by men
who profess themselves your admirers,
and not under the protection of your parents,
you are now at the most critical period
in the life of a woman.

Young, inexperienced, unsuspicious,
fond of flattery (as what woman is not),
she too often falls a victim to those worst of men
who, with the aid of oaths, protestations,
and promise of marriage,
seduce her from the paths of virtue,
rob her of her virginity,
and leave her to lament her credulity
in the most abject state of wretchedness,
deserted by her acquaintance,
reviled and scoffed at by her enemies,
a reproach to her friends,
a disgrace to her family,
and, far worse than all of these,
condemned by her own conscience!
The remainder of her life
must be miserable indeed.

If ever you find yourself in danger
of falling into this pit,
think only of the picture I have drawn
and you will shrink with horror
from the dreadful prospect,
and reflect with pleasing terror
on your happy deliverance
from the jaws of a monster so hideous.
Again, dear sister, let me advise you
not to throw yourself away.
You are yet very young,
neither ugly nor deformed,
of a creditable family,
and not entirely destitute of fortune.
Not that I would have you consider yourself
of more consequence than you are,
but I would deter you from doing
that which is beneath you.
Your very affectionate Brother,
Edward Bache.

Voyage

You would have liked, you said,
to live by the sea.
I think you had caught sight,
long ago, of the glass tower
in the midst of the sea,
and men on the tower
who did not answer your calling.
It was not really a house by the sea
you wanted, but embarkation.

Now at last you are committed
to the voyage. Rain-dark and spume
hide your dwindling ship.
In a shaft of storm-light
something gleams glassily to westward.
Let me think only
of landfall for you, and discount
the hundred stories of doom
bedevilling our ventures.

I see a hill rise out of the dark sea,
and you climbing to the tower.
I know your heart and know it set at last
towards the possibility of welcome.

Llyn y Fan Fach

Two women pick their way down from the lake,
sandals filling with sharp stones
or slithering on the hot grass verge.
"Not far now," they call. I can see
the black-red cliffs of the farther shore
rearing above knolls ahead. On the left,
far up to the craggy skyline,
parched pasture is stretched like yellow skin
on a fevered body. The sky
is a strident blue; there is no shade here,
no glint of healing water yet.

She has gone back long ago into the lake,
the lady of legend, taking
her mild cows and small snorting calves
and her own dark softness.
A gentleness three times struck with iron
is gone. The harsh track leads at last
to sombre cliffs, shadowed water.
On the shore I feel the breath of a breeze
from who knows what chill corridor.
Later, down the track, I call
to those who climb "Not far".

The Poem

In first light, cold
had its knives out. Even disaster
drew no crowd. The young policeman
seemed glad you stayed, although
you had not seen the car and did not know
the woman who, oddly tidy
except for smudges of dust and blood,
lay in the gutter.

(I think this is how you told it;
you are no longer here for me to ask.)

You thought that if her spirit were just then
to set out from humiliated flesh,
someone should be there, someone
who had chosen to wait. So,
till the ambulance came, two men,
one whose job it was and one who chose,
stood beside her.
                        Yet you could not accept
for that hurt body such a dog's death,
and in your mind kept crying "Don't die!",
unavailingly as, a few years on,
they cried who waited beside you.

Out of that acquiescent vigil
and silent protesting cry
you wanted to make a poem.
It would not get written.
There is just this thing that happened,
and your telling me of it
with a kind of puzzlement,
and in my mind the poem
neither of us will ever write.

Church in the Rain

Wrapped in rain the small church
stands high. There are no graves
on the north, the devil's side,
where blown soaking trees
transmit his cajoling cry
Let me in in in
To the south the sober congregation
of stones endures in grey uprightness.
The land slopes down into mist.

Inside the church I switch on lights,
shut the door on that crying in the trees.
Now there is the sweetness
of being dry when it rains,
having light after drearness.
A soft confusion of voices
laps up against this refuge.
Hide me, they say, comfort me
I want that which is no dream
That which I want is no dream
I want   I want

Thomas Powell died;
Catherine his mournful wife
cries and wants. Wine stands
in a vessel near the altar.
All ye who travail come
They are coming in from the rain
crying Save me, love me
and always that other wails
Let me in

As I leave, rain slacks. From the porch
I see the world in negative,
land eerily pale, sky black. Tonight
in my lighted room I feel the power
of that beleaguered place, miles away,
lightless in a night of rain and voices.
I want that which is no dream
That which I want is no dream
I want   I want
Let me in

Heavily falls, on and on, the rain

Fossils

We are finding fossils
in pebbles by the lake – minute skeletons,
inconceivably old. What such creatures
made of life is also inconceivable.
Robin is six, and prefers the plop
of pebbles into water, now,
and the skittering bounce of flat ones
over the surface, now.

Best are the small frogs, coral and green,
that half-hide in and out of weed
or sit in the shallows, placidly pulsing,
seeming to gaze intelligently up
at our refracted faces.
They are beautifully dressed in cold flesh,
aeons away from bony patterns
in layered rock; and better, I feel –
obstinately, like the child – better.

Friends' Room

They would make no claim for their quiet room.
Yet if there came a guilt long implanted,
ignorant of itself, bent on blackness,
here if anywhere it might be healed,
here where beyond the window
an apple-tree presses in –
soft-blossoming white forgiveness,
huge and branching, not content to stay
on the other side of glass.

The Ferret

Intent, they hardly noticed me,
the one child there.
I don't remember the ferret-man,
only the sly movement of hand to pocket,
the swift slinking beast thrust
into the hut, cleared of its hens.

Sounds, sights I recall
go quickly by in fragments,
like a not-too-explicit film
condensing violence – squeals,
blood on white, blood on grey,
bitten corpses glimpsed,
overlapping in a bucket:
the little killer retrieved,
tucked away, still splashed with red.

What I remember clearly
and with a living repulsion
is the woman, grey-haired, red-eyed,
in a long white apron, who screamed and wept,
laughed and screamed, throwing her apron
up over her head, but not going,
staying there, looking again, screaming again.

It was the rhythmic sweep of the apron
that frightened me, the disappearance
of her long face with its wet red eyes –
that, and the hideous sound of her horror.

Later, I tried to tell, and was not heard.
"She cried," was all I kept saying.
They laughed, puzzled, soothing me
about the shrill necessary
bloody deaths that had not appalled me,
promising me the ferret had gone away.

Hawthorn at Digiff

When I was a child, hawthorn
was never brought into our house.
It was godless to throw a pinch
of spilled salt, or dodge ladders,
yet no-one ever carried in
the doomy sweetness of red may or white.

Down there by the river,
shivering with heat, is Digiff,
a house full of hawthorn. The tree
grows in the midst of it, glowing
with pale pink blossom, thrusting
through gaps that were windows,
reaching up where no roof
intervenes between hearth and sky.

On the hill, sun has hardened
old soggy fields below the bluebell woods.
Rusty wire sags from rotten posts.
Outcrops, couchant dinosaurs, share
rough comfort with a few unshorn sheep.
Below, gardens have left their mark.

I bring a thought into this day's light
of Esther and Gwen, paupers:
Rhys and Thomas, shepherds: John Jones,
miner of copper and lead:
who lived here and are not remembered,
whose valley is re-translated
by holiday bathers across the river,
lying sun-punched: by me:
by men who keep a scatter of sheep
on the old by-takes.

At Digiff is hawthorn on hearth and bed-place.
Seen close, the tree is flushed
with decay. Sick lichened branches
put out in desperate profusion
blossom that hardly knows
an hour of whiteness before slow dying
darkens it. This is that glowing tree
of doom and celebration,
whose cankered flowers I touch
gently, and go down to the ford.

Lichen, Cladonia Fimbriata

This little scaly thing,
fibrous lichen, taker of peat-acid
and the rotten juice of dead trees,
grows lowly, slowly, on bog-earth
or the scant soil of crevices,
and holds up to the air its fruit
in tiny fantastic goblets.

Might not this pallid creeping thing,
that needs for food only the sour,
sparse and corrupt, be late to go? –
too small and too tenacious
to be torn off by the dusty wind,
and offering in final celebration
its little tainted chalices?

Wings

"You are one who would fly
if she had wings," said the woman
peddling at sunset cotton, plastic pegs
and flattery. Yet it was she,
surely, deserved the words
with their romantic shadows, she
who gripped the world as a falcon the fist.

Unsurprised, with small thanks,
she took the coins and turned away.
Now that her dark shape was gone
from the step, nothing obscured
the silhouetted hill, the red sky
promising sublime weather
for some inaccessible morning,
taunting the whole clip-wing world.

Train to the Sea

When she was old, contented,
I think, with her inland home,
she said "One of these mornings
I'm going to get on a train
by myself, and go to the sea."
It became just something she would say,
repeated with no urgency,
little conviction. No-one felt any need
to help her set out on that small adventure.
No-one thought she would do it, or even
that she truly wanted to go.

Yet after she died, I found her list
of trains to the sea, crumpled a bit
and thumbed, as if she had often
peered at it, making her plans.
But always in the end it seemed
a formidable, rash and lonely thing,
that little journey, and she calmed
her heart with small domestic things,
or saw rain coming, or heavy heat, and stayed.

Turning Inland

Hard to leave you on the cold sands,
your back to slow-shifting dunes,
waiting, your gaze on the sea's patterns.

Hard to think you not alone;
if there are others on that beach
they are not such as I can see.

Hard to know it good that I
should turn inland, keeping the gift
of your paradoxical presence.

Pausing

What do they make of it? Down they come
from the hill, damp maps flapping, anoraks
brightly outfacing the weather, walking-boots
dark with bog-water. Suddenly
the sun comes out; hoods are pushed back,
laces loosened. Here it is, the valley
they headed for, spying on the map
slackening contours, green-edged meanders,
and the thin line of road beyond
plunging on into brown, more brown.
Here it is; their most wishful imaginings
prove true. Happily they pause
by the stream. Soon to be gone, they need
put nothing to the test. Stepping out,
they will be able to say,
luxuriating, "If we could only stay!"

Slate Quarry, Penceulan

I had known the quarry for years –
dark hills of broken slate: round hole,
high up, of an adit: a black
unfenced shaft down by the river:
and, reassuringly, above it all
a strip of untroubled green catching the sun.

When I spoke of the place to a man
who well knew it, that bland field
was the danger he warned of –
not slipping slate, not the tunnel's whisper
of shift and sag. The high field,
said he, spoke no word of its peril.
He had seen horses, dogs, men
skeltering along it, and no harm done.

But he had been inside the hill. He drew
no chart; from his words I read
the unfading map spread in his mind.
I know the three-branched tunnel now,
the water-barrier, the fall-blocked road,
the third way with its rusty rails
reddish in torchlight, opening out
into a chamber whose functional hugeness
amazes, whose dark hollowness
rears up close under sunny grass.

My mind makes a tree, rising out of the dark
of that hidden hall, breaking the shell
of the hill, flowering high in the air,
binding blackness to light. Its petals cling
in the manes of horses that innocently go
galloping on the green brittle hill.

Solstice

December moon swells:
Virgo rises in the east.
Behind early curtains we hide
from gentle exacting light
in controllable brightness,
and tame to tinsel patterns
the immortality-tree.
We are as adamantly shut,
as helpless, as the solstice-door,
that will not escape
the imminent shattering of locks
at the push of a child's hand.

from *Selected Poems* (1992)
(new poems section)

Breaking Bowls

The Maya broke bowls,
smashed weapons, shredded clothes,
killed them, to let their souls go free
into the owner's eternity.

It seems less naïve a concept
than stocking a tomb with toys,
mirrors, cooking-pots, or a ship
with gold armour.
          We crunch and stumble
through a dark archway, over shards,
splinters, rags of a life, taking
(as we were warned) nothing with us,
except an idea of completeness, an intuition
of light, perhaps a welcome
for the little souls of things
flying free to meet us.

"I'm here to get away from myself"

(Hotel guest)

She takes a climbing track
scented, shut in, by fir and pine.
From a high corner, landslip
has churned a chaotic ride
all the way down to the valley floor,
making a vertical stripe
of wide-world brightness. Afterwards,
higher, again the forest closes in,
its night of naked underwood
lit here and there by streaks of sun.

Insistent comes the scent
of hot needles, opening cones.
Insistent comes her heartbeat, like the pad
of the draggled old bitch-hound, self,
that rejected slinks at her heel,
humbly, relentlessly following
for the small accepting pat
disgust will not let her give.

Carreg yr Adar (Rock of the Birds)

Jettisoned in molinia by the river
near the Rock of the Birds,
the rags of his body had long begun
their measured rot towards
clean bone, blown dust
when after weeks another walker
came over the moors.

A jet-plane momentarily
tore silence open.
The skeletal dog, still on guard,
did not flinch. At last
it was coaxed away.
Memory stayed inaccessible
in its head's cave –
a howling song in an alien mode,
still faintly echoing.

Soon the body
was gathered up and gone.
New grass would grow, knowing
only air, rain, dew, the excrement
and paw-press of the hill's creatures.

***

The Rock of Birds juts out
from eastern slope to stream,
half-bars the valley. A stony path
creeps round it by the river.
To the north, feeder-streams debouch
in a waste of stones.
Little crumbled houses
are shapes of an old summer life,
dairies in no rich pasture,
no green idyll.

One is a perfect oval,
an open eye questioning heaven.

***

Last night, summer rain
soaked our bedplace. He laughed,
pulling me to him. But this morning
the smoored fire was out,
peat-ash a mess of unchancy black,
and my butter puddled with rain.

He was at work all day
at his bunching and patching
with the reeds. The cattle
cropped the grudging grass.
I left the hut,
searching for stumps of bogwood,
strength for the re-lit fire.
There was a man
walking away downstream,
dog at heel. Nor man nor dog
seemed like any I knew;
but they were far at the edge of sight,
and soon gone.

Tonight we lie warm, dry,
under the mended thatch.
The butter is pearled
only with its own sweet sweat.
I have woken, hearing faintly
a howling far downstream.
I lie closer to my sleeping man,
warm, but with open eyes
questioning the night.

***

Here are shifting streams,
stones studding old riverbeds:
named streams
dropping, dawdling, dropping
down rocky channels
out of the moors, ancient lands
of stone-heavers, mound-men.
By streams of the Bull, the Crow,
Sow, Curlew, Wolf-bitch, Stag,
priests of the mound-men danced
unsparing strength of bird and animal
into the tribe, that it might live.

***

I wear the feathered cloak
I am beak-faced.
I range the valley
to tear and gorge.
I do not spare the half-born lamb
or the still-breathing ewe.
I do not spare the body of a man.

***

From the small town he turned
south into the hills. The dog
ran ahead, or padded at heel,
sometimes pushing its long nose
against his hand.

          Their passing
was a hardly perceptible
imperfection in silence.
Once a jet tore through the sky. Once
came the rasping cry of a crow,
calling its mate to carrion.

Unhurried, unfaltering, man and dog
followed their appointed way
across the hills, over the little streams,
down-valley to the Rock of the Birds.

Leaving

They carried her from the door
down the path. The stretcher jolted
at the small gate, but she kept quiet.
All the way to the ambulance that waited
at the end of the narrow track,
she stared up at branches
dancing backwards on a windy sky.

She had been alone for years,
the trees her love, her fear,
her endless conversation.
Outside, the world changed
and did not change. In pictures
she saw it bleed. Around the house
the year's autumnal blood
seeped from tree to ground,
and spring's new combatant growth
played politics of survival.

Branches blurred now above her.
The wide sky she had forgotten
came nearer; millions of unseen worlds
swung into patterns of dance.
Into those huge compulsive rhythms
step by jarring step she was borne on.

Earth Tremor

There was a muffled sound, like a train
tunnelling through the hill.
Daffodils in a vase on the table
shuddered for long seconds, long enough
for incredulity to crystallize.

As the small world stabilized
came, illogically, a sense that this
had been something incurred
five minutes, five years ago,
by doing or not doing – a step
not taken, decision bedevilled;
as if it were better to feel guilty
and thankful than know fire-hearted earth
ungovernable, even here.
                    The still daffodils,
never so soft, so crisp, so yellow,
shone, reprieved.

Bookmark

A blurred snapshot cut to bookmark size
shows a small naked boy, a girl
seal-sleek in her prized swimsuit,
scrambling up a stream. Fern and foxglove
shade and dwarf them. Clutching slippery rocks
they lean forward in a never-passing
moment of effort. Ahead, the sunny grass
they reached and long ago forgot
waits for the press of their wet bodies.

The slip of fuzzy colour-print
already droops dog-eared. Keep it
in a dull book on the top shelf,
almost as safe, almost as hidden
as handgrip in rock, footstep in water,
shadow in springing grass.

Oil-spill, 1991

The cormorant can heave itself
from the black beach, over the low wall,
and run about the tarmac till it dies.
Or it can let the thick strange sea
slurp at it till it sags and dies.

The camera zooms in
on punk-spikes of oiled feathers
and the no-understanding,
no-reproach, of round unblinking eyes
that say nothing, simply see,
and see now this last thing.

from: Sources
1. Probate: to Thomas Price

You were here, Thomas,
two and a half centuries back,
lordling of a stony acreage:
in your plain rectangle of house,
your nurturing barns,
your yard where the wind caught its breath
and bore on down-valley.

Fatherless, only son,
you wielded a brother's potestas
over your sisters' likings.
Barely yourself of age, you were set
to rule their sullen ripening.

I riffle the writings, searching
for a word more of you.
You were here, Thomas;
I will set down such small dry words
as I find of you, proclaim
against the brag of chaos
a tiny clarity.

Now! now! as you knew it
comes that catch in the wind
and the long howl of its dying.

2. Chancery: Opening Music

Long parchments and limp inky scraps
corded together, the documents wait.
I smooth and sort, remembering
suddenly a long-forgotten shiver
and challenge, new piano-pieces
my teacher used to open for me,
smoothing the stiff pages;
and the music starting in my head
before a note was played.

Somewhere in this dusty bundle
he waits, old Benjamin, crusty and half-drunk
in his Radnorshire kitchen.
                              "Did he throw the will
on the fire, and did you pluck it off?" –
"No", says the widow, badgered
by the Commissioners (making her mark
on the hesitant deposition), "not on the fire
as they aver, yet he did throw it on the floor,
having cut off the seal; and then again
picked it up and pinned it together
and bade me keep it locked in the coffer
till it should be needed".
"But did he take a disgust,
a disinheriting disgust, to Charles his heir?"
"Not a disgust", she says, "yet he was somewhat
in a fret, and I would not bring the will
that night, when he was in liquor;
but next day he did as I have said".

This music has waited for me to smooth its pages
and stumble into halting interpretation
of tentative harmonies, broken phrasing,
less-than-perfect cadences. In my head
I hear what my best skill can never show –
the true notes, played with love.

3. Recusant Records: Sectarian

I, Gunter of Gwenddwr,
being of the Old Faith, and for that
much hedged and strictured
and my lands bled of just profit,
have still the advowson
of that heretical conventicle
they call their Parish Church –
church once indeed, but now defiled
by false opinion and mock sacrament.
I catch at a name, give them one
Walter Powell. Up goes their shriek
and cavil – Powell utters no Lord's Prayer,
reads them no Gospel. They will have Prydderch,
Thomas Prydderch or none. Fools!
As though Powell or Prydderch
or any other from the rabble
of bastard ministers unblest
by Christ's apostles could serve
to pull them heavenwards! What care I
for their lamentable capers,
their clownish clerks? One of my bull beasts
would be good enough for them.

(Note: The last sentence of the poem was actually spoken by
Bodenham Gunter, or so says the county historian.)

Resurrection Angels

(Kilvert was told that people used to come to the Wild Duck
Pool on Easter morning "to see the sun dance and play in the
water and the angels who were at the Resurrection playing
backwards and forwards before the sun".)

These were not troubling the waters
to bring healing. They were serving
no purpose. After the watch at the tomb,
the giving of good news, they were at play.
To and fro went the wings, to and fro
over the water, playing before the sun.

Stolid-seeming villagers stared
enchanted, watching sun dance and play,
light-slivers splinter water's dark.
In dazzle they half-saw
great shining shapes swoop frolicking
to and fro, to and fro.

                    This much was shared,
expected; day and place had their
appropriateness, their certainties.
The people had no words to tell
the astonishment, the individual bounty –
for each his own dance in the veins,
brush of wings on the soul.

Emu's Egg

Trudging through rain along the windy hill
to pull a snarled-up lamb, whistle the dogs
to their flat-out looping of the ewes,
he nursed the notion of Australia –
heat, space, a chance of more
than his hard-earned Breconshire pittance.
Idea became plan, was told,
marvelled at, acted on. He was best friend
to my old neighbour's grandfather,
turned to him for help – a horse and cart
to Liverpool. Northwards they rattled,
through Builth, Newtown, Welshpool. At Liverpool
came a fraught moment. "John", he said,
tears not far, "John, sell the horse and cart,
come with me!" For a moment
that far-off sun shone for his friend too,
coaxing; then it was dimmed
by green damp, more deeply penetrating.
"No", said John, "I can't, I can't"; turned south
through Welshpool, Newtown, Builth again.

John was dead by the time
a letter came, and an Australian parcel,
exotic, unique – an emu's egg,
black, the size (his children said)
of two teacups put together.
It stayed at the farm for years,
then got broken. For a while
they saved the fragments of shell; the story
lasted a little longer. Unlikely transmitter,
I set it down, feeling perhaps for both
brave dreamer and chicken-hearted friend –
one who forced a dream to live, and one
who missed for ever his black two-teacup egg.

Llanfihangel Abergwesyn

Some still remember the rose-window
shining through dusk, the bells
that played hymn-tunes, the one
that tolled for the valley's dead.
Splendid Victorian folly, the church itself
lived less than a century. Soft stone
sopped up the endless rain. Above cross-point
of nave and transept, heavy tower
made an infinitesimal shift, chancel arch
moved a millimetre out of true.
In the pulpit, an intermittent drip
punctuated sermons. Whisper by whisper
flaking began, softest of plaster-fall
from pillar and wall, drift of dust
on chaliced wine. Then as a doomed mind,
whose tiny eccentricities have given
little unease, suddenly lurches to grosser
irrationality, the building shed
a first sodden chunk of facing stone,
and was put away.
Damp barricaded silence lasted
till the slow thudding months of demolition,
the final blasting of the tower.
Grass, yew-trees, graves remain,
and in a few old minds regret
no longer sharp, but steady as rain
that brought down stone and fed the flood of grass.

Catching Up

The grubby room is almost empty.
Her chair is an island on bare floor.
She is not poor. She has chosen in age
to throw away a life's dead weight.
Rugs, rosewood, silver, translucent bowls
have all gone (to the unworthy, some think).
On her narrow bed, a mound shifts,
furtively, under the greyish cover, mews.

I remember her immaculate –
brown hair scraped back, pinned relentlessly:
eyes sharply judging: tenderness
kept for pampered, pampering gewgaws.
Now white rough-cut hair
hangs softly round her gentler face;
eyes are young, see far; grimy hands
unclench and lie content.

On a tiny television screen,
into loving dark of summer woods
children run through meadow grass.
It has taken years to catch up;
she sees them just ahead,
the width of a field away.

Green Man at the Bwlch

For a week or more
some baffling serendipity
has brought him to me
in books, journals, photographs –
a splay-mouthed face,
flesh shared with leaves.

Now on a remote pass above trees
of two Radnor valleys
I come to this ancient place –
cruck house half-crumbled, lovingly encased
by scaffolding and plastic sheets, cocoon
in which goes on the work of rebirth.
He is here too.

In a central room, on the beam
over the great hearth, royally
he spreads his mouth-borne branches,
meets my unsurprised eyes.
Here is an abyss, like Nietzsche's,
into which if I look long
I find it looking into me.

The terror is in his utter
neutrality. Yet somewhere
in his kingdom of possibilities
is a tree whose leaves give shelter,
whose boughs know songs, whose sap
flows gold through our veins.

Valley-before-Night

(The upper Camarch Valley in the old parishes of Abergwesyn
and Llanafan used to be a community of some sixteen farms.
Most of the houses are ruined or demolished. When this poem
was written Llednant was still farmed and Coedtrefan was
occupied – Robin, Hazel, Tomos and Gwyn were the only chil-
dren who lived in the valley. The local name for the Camarch
Valley is *Cwm-cyn-Nos* – the before-night valley, Valley-before-
Night. *Cyheuraeth* – howling (a death-omen, auditory equiva-
lent of the corpse-candle). *Dechreunos* – beginning-of-night (a
custom prevalent here till the second world war).

***

"Why Cwm-cyn-Nos?" No-one's answer
seemed complete. "It was best
to be home in that valley, or out of it,
before night", one said, adding "perhaps".
Another, "There was never a road
up the Camarch, till the Forestry came".
One man quietly said "That is a dark valley".

***

Looking down from the pass
I saw the valley shiver with light.
Even swathes of spruce, obscuring
paths, fields, old stones,
rose quivering into sun. The river danced
with brilliant daytime candles, omens
of nothing but heat. Yet even then
(was it because I knew that name?)
there seemed a darkness of obliquity,
enigma. Outlines blurred,
as in a photograph of fir-tree tops,
that always looks shaken. For a moment
I read the place as a cryptogram
for danger. Soon the fancy was gone. I saw

only innocent light brimming a green bowl,
and time on time in a subaqueous dance.

***

Griffith Thomas of Cefn Gilfach went to Rhaeadr
market to buy iron pots for his son's marriage-gift.
Returning over the moors in heavy summer rain, at
the ford over the Camarch below his house he was
swept away by a sudden wild up-swelling of the
river.
Coming home late one evening from shepherding,
William Arthur of Blaencwm saw a light dance on the
river between Carregronw and Fedw, and hurried on.
Near that spot the next day was found the body of
Griffith Thomas.

***

Robin

They sounded the death
in daytime night of the trees.
"Can I go?" he had asked.
We stood by the fence,
watching him run down the field.
Alders by the river hid him; then
there again was the red shirt,
small on the farther hill, as his hurtling rush
dwindled to a laboured climb.
A few riders distantly manoeuvered,
scattering over the hillside:
dogs arrowed towards the wood,
disappeared inside.
Soon came that horn-call;
suddenly all was still,
horses and riders enchanted
into a triangle inverted.

Near its apex, a red splash
marked where the boy stood,
motionless too, facing the trees.
Only the river ran on.
We could not hear the worrying,
tearing, of the ritual kill.
What he saw, heard, we do not know.
He came back chastened, with little to say.
The younger ones jostled and laughed;
soon he was laughing with them,
the still moment with its burden of death
given to the river flowing always
through night at the back of the mind.

***

Thomas Thomas of Cluniau died far from the
Camarch, at Merthyr Cynog on the Epynt hills,
and was carried on a wagon for burial at
Abergwesyn. One night when he lay still
breathing, waiting his time, his corpse-candle
was seen, going home before him.

***

Who saw the corpse-lights dance
for the death of the farms?

***

Four miles up from Dôlaeron bridge
Cedney flows in, on its bank Pencae.
Twenty years back the shepherd Evan
spread starched white fire of tablecloth
to light the room with ceremony for me,
set china from long-ago markets.
Eleven young ones had grown in that house;

two were left, old men. The valley
had scampered with children.
Only the river ran and chattered now.
Two years ago, he said,
a girl on a palamino
had ridden upstream: my daughter.
I felt filaments of time
bind me to her memory and his,
all of us into the valley story.
I left when dark was a hint only,
a growing scent of hay and river-damp,
and did not see him again.

***

Hazel

"He won't go!" she grumbled,
ineffectually kicking
the fat pony's sides, her blue gaze
muddled with tears. "Don't drag his mouth",
her mother called. "Take him off the track,
up through the trees". Later
they burst from the wood, chased
alongside us, past us, over the grass.
"He's cantering!" she shouted,
joyful eight-year-old centaur,
part at last of the godling,
filled with beauty and power, her fair hair
flopping, all life riding her way.
Night sent its outriders of cloud
to escort her. She stooped
to the pony's neck in an embrace,
cajoled him to the track, rode home.

***

"When I was a girl at Pencae",
the woman said, "my mother
would send me down to Fedw to sleep,
for company for the wife there. Sometimes
her man worked away from home;
she didn't like to be there at night
with only her little ones. I would hurry
down the track, to get there by dark.
She would stir the logs to warm us,
and for light. We ate our food
by the fire, and went to bed
with the children, together,
in a long room in the roof.
We could hear owls, and wind
loosening the birch-leaves; they would go
creeping and dancing over the roof.
But we slept; we were all together.
In the morning I would go home.
My mother would look at me, sharp-like,
and ask, "*A oedd popeth yn iawn yn y Fedw?*
– Was it all right at the Fedw?"

***

Morgan Dafydd of Pencae died from a wound,
falling from his horse on to a little dagger
which he had with him for an evil purpose.
At two o'clock in the morning of that day, Rhys
Rowland had seen a coffin made of light, stand-
ing outside Morgan's house. Meeting him later,
Rhys warned him, but in vain.

***

Tomos

"No!" he shouts, asleep, in the early hours.
"No!" meeting comfort with anger and fear.
Only his father can help, prising him
from a snarl of blankets, carrying
the tense resistant two-year-old downstairs
and out into moonlight. "Look, Tomos,
there's the moon" – and slowly
he slackens and nestles, even smiles,
finding this valley night kinder
than the dreamed one, where who know what
old savageries had claimed him
as victim, participant. By day
he is extrovert, charmer,
paying with small change of smiles
for the fears his daring creates. Only tiredness
tames him. Patching his scratches
we guess at hurts only dark hours reveal,
and which the pharmacopeia of love
must surely hold a salve to heal.

***

Here at Sychnant, where now is only the skinny
disproportion of a broken house, lived the
slate-quarry bailiff. Here died six-year-old
William Garibaldi Williams, and went over the
pass to lie with others of Cwm-cyn-Nos in the
chapel-yard of Pantycelyn.

***

Under the flagstone by the door
of Gilwern was a ghost in a box,
marauding spirit of a Scot
killed for his pack and his cash.

154

After years, there were rumours
of sounds in the hall, on the stairs.
Men said he had swelled in his rage,
burst free. One day he would choose
his victim. There is no charmer now
to catch and box him.
New owner, summerer, can you repair
moaning hall, groaning stair?

***

Dôlcegyrn: walls by the river, an old tale
of a church St Michael rejected,
whisking stones away by night.
The known was a cottage
with a plum-tree. Pencae children,
on their way down-valley,
would thieve and dodge,
escaping sticky, cock-a-hoop,
pockets squashy with plums.
Dusk holds the swish and pad
of small feet sneaking past
in a hurry, on the long path home.

***

Gwyn

The small grey rabbit executes
an improbable twisting skip
and vanishes behind the sofa.
The baby on the floor
is totally given up to laughter.
Seven months old, native of the valley,
he is happy, humorous,
except when a pain, or hunger,

briefly darkens his life.
His round intent eyes fix constantly
upon the world's myriad appearances,
and feed his brain to satiation.
He does not yet know
ordinary from strange;
he is not vulnerable
to the ambiguities of dusk.
He rolls on his back, smiling up
at plants on the sill, staring
at leaf-shapes against the darkening panes.

***

The many stones at Pantycelyn
grow hard to read, as moss and lichen
impose their freer patterns
on flowing script, grey wings and flowers.

***

Isaac, son of Isaac Thomas of Fedw, died in February
1812, aged four. His sister Margaret died next
Christmas Day, aged one year. John Arthur of
Carregronw died in 1866 aged ninety-two. Edward
Lewis of Pencae, shepherd and poet, called Iorwerth
Camarch, died in 1947 aged sixty-four.

***

Who heard the *cyheuraeth* for the doomed farms?
Who heard the *cyheuraeth* pass along the valley?

***

The last tenant of Llednant
is old. The Forestry watches him
as a buzzard a failing beast.
Each day now, with its ritual
of feeding, herding, fencing,
is a small battle won
in the war he must lose.
More than his life will end;
he knows it. "Tomorrow"
means only the next day.
He tends on still unplanted fields
creatures who make no plans,
and fills his tired days
with the quiet of their unawareness.

***

Dechreunos

A woman trundles her baby home
as winter sun dips; a little boy
trudges, hand on the pushchair.
Soon, two homing from school
are voices in the wood,
shapes on the track,
squabbling, laughter, at the door.
When dark comes, the house
spills light; on it float
shadows, stretching, retracting.
A man returns. Briefly, the door
lets light gush out. Then
a family is enclosed in light,
the house in the valley night.

Out of the dark they came,
Camarch's people, for *dechreunos*.
Work ended with daylight; then
each night one house,
one only up-valley and down,
would fill itself with light
(every candle lit, every lamp)
for neighbours' sheltered hour
of talk in a luxury of light.
Along darkening paths they came.
Each time the door was opened,
against outflowing of light
a shape of darkness moved in,
silhouette vanishing into light.

Coedtrefan keeps *dechreunos*
for people of invisible houses.
Dark finds its entrance, speaks
to dark of each heart.
Light pours like benediction.
Hands salving present hurts
soothe timeless agonies to sleep.
On spilt light, shadows stretch and shrink.
The children sleep. Beyond an unseen field
Camarch whirls its flotsam on
over chafed stones: flows free of time.

from *The Fluent Moment* (1996)

The Fluent Moment

Against an inner wall of the small church
leans a symbol-stone, encapsulating
all things known, at rest. Sober-faced Sun,
rayed with crisp flames, is King of a static world.

But in the porch, ivy has climbed
right through the walls, insinuating
tough stems into crevices above the arch;
and flows high up in dark luxuriance,
forcing an over-shoulder glance, a thought
of all things built to fall, falling to rise.

The future has been and has been.
There is a movement here like Escley stream
that down from slopes of Cefn arrives
and in the same fluent moment leaves.

The Swift

There were prayers about famine. After,
lowering hymnbooks, children laughed,
their wildness released by a swift
that came dipping through the door,
sweeping to and fro, low over pews,
from font to altar and back.
For adults, dark rhythms of flight heightened,
not hid, pictures lodged in reluctant minds.

Up, up flew the swift. It would stay
for days unreachable, fall starved. Silhouetted,
clinging to the east window's topmost pane,
it drooped black angled wings symmetrically
over glories of suffering and triumph,
seeming to offer mutely, in doomed grace,
blackest of shadows for images of shelter.

Siân Fach

"Little Jane", they called her, "Siân fach".
"A proud little woman",
said her English daughter-in-law,
who never felt well in Conwy –
something to do, she thought, with the hills,
too near, too big, stealing the best of the air.
Something to do with Siân fach, too,
the little spendthrift widow
petted and subsidized
by her four sons, and slaved for
by her one resentful daughter.

Always a huddle of Welsh
chuntering in corners, family talk
never fully translated, sounding
crisis-laden. Little Jane was polite
to the foreign bride, speaking to her
occasionally, in careful English –
an aristo attempting patois
for the benefit of a well-disposed
but regrettable connection,
of a lesser breed.

I have a photograph of Siân,
still dark-haired, stiffly trim in black.
Small, old and queenly, chin uptilted,
she sits throned on a wooden chair
at the top of stone steps outside
her ancient house. Standing at her side,
looking apologetic, is a courtier
halfway back into favour, the son
who brought home a stranger.

His bride, of course,
is not in the picture. If there was
any contest, it is she, I suppose,
who won, remaining a visitor only,
and not a frequent one; seeing to it
that her family's roots were plunged
into warm coaly earth of the South,
with its more manageable hills
and uncensorious jumble of language.

Siân, you died before I was old enough
to be taken North. What would you make
of a granddaughter tripped
by the rocks of your language,
a great-grandson not of the North
yet bonded to its mountains?
Apart from that photograph,
all I ever had of you
was an ormolu clock that got lost or sold,
and whatever sawdusty treasures
I dipped from the mysterious
lucky tub of your genes.

Let us not judge each other.
If I put away your photograph,
it's not to disown proud little Siân,
only to keep from fading,
another year or two,
that record, that faint sepia memory.

Away from Home

The Irish doctor and his wife
lived their expatriate rôle
to the last quirk and syllable.
Seven years old, I could see
but not define their strangeness.
Not knowing brandy, I had no name
for that dominant note in the close
heavy-perfumed room.

            I liked the parrot,
its slowly-tilting head, its aged critical eye,
half-human raucous talk.

            I liked the doctor,
who said little, chewed on his pipe, stared out
(sadly, I thought) over back-to-back rows
to the hills.

            Most, I liked his wife, her desperate
un-Welsh, un-English chatter, the one curler
often forgotten among tight rolls
of shiny black hair, her startling beads,
the way she would tip a bottle
over her teacup, turn on
a scrapy gramophone, and plumply jig,
reaching out to her husband, who made
only a small disclaiming gesture.

I think that even then I sensed
the doctor and his wife were away from home
for ever (since home, if they returned,
would not be what they wanted), and that they
knew this, and could not be healed.
I sipped the too-sugary tea, and tried to dance.

from: Six Houses

Kilvert Visits Penoyre

"Only twenty-five bedrooms", said the diarist,
disappointed with their small size
and the darkness of the billiard room.
He didn't see it at its best (the old Colonel
was five years dead, fading impoverished
at the Bear in Brecon; and the whole place
was peeling). Why couldn't he talk about
the views? – east to the Black Mountains,
westward to Usk and more hills, south
to wooded Benni and the Beacons? All that
mattered more, didn't it, than deal pillars
(that should have been marble) and the rest
of the "sham hollow work" (fun for the Colonel,
and crumbling anyway by 1870)?

Down fields and a shady ride he found the lake,
one end reed-choked, the other channelled
towards the river, and "rippling heavy and muddy"
like local stories. It was the fishing-lodge
that took his fancy; he was disapproving
and fascinated. "Wild strange work"! He told
only of carriages waiting all night,
bursts of fireworks over the boats on the lake,
dancing in the ballroom until morning.
The rest stayed in his mind. Still,
what he left out could hardly have surprised,
however mixed his feelings, a man
who knew the "angel satyr" on the hill.

(Kilvert's diary entry for 20 June 1871 is "An angel satyr
walks these hills".)

from: Land

1. Sioned

Before I took her to wife
I judged the land by yield, its contours
as workable or not, and all it grew
food, shelter or nuisance.

Then she came, smiling, over my threshold.
Sioned, Sioned, said the wind,
that I had never listened to before
except for warning of storm.
From the tyddyn's grudging windows,
creaking door, now when I looked I saw.

Red-brown leaves, that had been nothing
but hint of winter, were warm with her hair's colour;
and in spring the useless bluebells,
that fed no stock, and sent my sled askew,
were for joy now, being her eyes
beneath my gaze.

He had two years, our son, until
his playtime ended, and he lay
fevered and wasting, drooling out
the sips of cawl or milk his mother held
to his white lips. Those weeks
before he died seemed longer
than all his tiny life till then.

She has a way now, on the warmest day
or by the hot winter hearth, of chafing
hand on hand, as though wringing them,
or as if some chill can never let her go.
Stiffly, in duty, she moves from task to task,
lies in our bed.
Sioned, Sioned, cries the wind over the hill,
where close among grasses bluebell leaves
wait for the spring.

167

2. Landscape with Figures

Behind the house loomed crags of a ravine.
A breeze, shifting, carried watery echoes.
Everything was pervaded by the valley's
extreme, uncompromising beauty. I thought
that there, whatever in the weave
might be harsh, twisted, disproportionate,
must stretch and blend into a balanced pattern.

One man I met there then is dead.
Invaded by a dark he could not speak of,
he cut his life away. The farmer stayed.
Skilled with the whittling-knife, in solitude
he wakes from wood the beasts asleep in it.
Weather and men he meets with taciturn
competence, keeping his counsel, never
risking unguarded boundaries.

Sometimes I see them waving me goodbye,
standing on the yard, their valley lit
superbly by fitful sun; and now see too
how down the ravine white mist would roll
like mercy to cover the suffering house,
and the land's beauty, that was not enough.

3. January Road

Fog and frost are forecast. Cold
has already deepened. Bare hill,
forested hill, rear into mist.
Up the farm road go Landrover,
grey digger with red arm bent back,
blue pick-up. Murky air deceives,
imposing strange perspectives;
from across the stream, climbing vehicles
are magnified to closeness, having startling
immediacy, their colour changing
this weather of despair.

The Landrover is gone
into encroaching white; foot by foot
digger vanishes, like a python's prey;
noisily, little pick-up follows.
Over the mountain the last curl of road
to a ruined house and its living pastures
will be made before cold clenches
too rigidly for prising.

                    Ragged-fringed,
mist drifts lower. From far within it comes,
faintly now, purposeful hum of motors,
long crunch of wheels, clunk of shifted stone,
undaunted music of the bright machines,
already journeying into spring.

Bluetit Feeding

Early at the window in starved winter
a little knot of energies, a beaky hunger
fluffed and sleeked, taps, prises
unsucculent scraps of cracked putty,
swallows with a ripple of tiny throat.

Behind it climbs a bleak pale hill
stained with rust of December bracken.
White morning moon is barely seen
on hardly darker sky that seems
opaque, a barrier against pressure
of immensities. Imperceptibly
the chill day flows out to black deeps.

The bluetit pauses in its arid feeding,
flirts a crisp wing. Half-handful of warmth,
it stays for a moment still,
compellingly centre-stage, diminishing
to a backdrop the hill, dull morning sky,
pale echo of moon, black vertiginous
trenches of space-ocean, myriads
of molten and frozen, dying and rising worlds.

Deer in Wyre Forest

(for Amy)

We went into the forest, looking for deer.
Even when we started, light was failing;
but this was her home patch – she held my hand
politely, not for reassurance.
She knew the landmarks: the huge cleared swathe
where a pipe-line struck out cross-country,
the treetop hide, the side-path into dark
(a good place for toadstools).
                              When we reached
the observation post, it was closed.
We peered through glass at posters,
half-visible, and across the glade
to the further tree-fringe, hoping
for the lithe wariness of homing deer.

As we turned to go, rain-clouds
thickening dusk, a flick of movement
caught us. We looked back. Over the clearing,
dim at the forest edge, was a shape, shadow,
a thing poised, a presence that distantly
skittered and snuffled.
A deer, we said, and set out content
for the dark return between dense trees
to the lights of her father's car.

I can't find that walk in my diary.
For years she may not find it in memory –
perhaps not till she is old
will something startle one day from hiding
the shapes of that evening. There, suddenly,
will be the doe in the dusky glade,
secret at the forest verge, homing.

Through Binoculars

I turn the knurled ring; the top field
blurs, sharpens. Identified,
a buzzard stares from its post
as if into my eyes.
That is another country,
hill rising more steeply,
woods massing darkly
in unfamiliar proportion.

Always the lens, plastic or glass,
the tough jelly of the eye,
the mind's distortion.
Through my binoculars,
my imperfect eyes,
my struggling mind,
I stare; with illusory
complicity, the buzzard's eyes
meet mine, as if we shared,
one moment, a view of the world.
Then with slow power its wings
lift; it soars beyond my lenses' reach.

Hare at Pennant

(The ancient life-symbol of the Hare became debased over the centuries. One of its later manifestations, the Trickster, is in this poem identified with the hare saved by Saint Melangell from the hounds of Prince Brochwel in an ancient Latin ms copied in the 17th century.)

I Hare have been the clever one,
up to my tricks, always a winner,
fooling man and beast – but not now,
not you, pretty lady, holy one.
You untwist my deviousness.
I huddle at your feet
in your garments' folds,
and am simple hare, fool hare, hunted hare.
I have doubled and doubled,
am spent, blown, not a trick left
to baffle pursuers.
A leap of despair
has brought me to you.

Cudd fi, Melangell,
Monacella, hide me!

***

"Seize him!" I cried to my hounds
(the best, I had thought, in all
my princedom of Powys).
But each time I chivvied them on,
the fools came squealing and squelking back.
So I rode into tanglewood,
my huntsmen after me,
the wretched scruff-hounds skulking off;
and she was there in the glade,
still as an image, still
as her carved Christ on his cross.
I pictured her alone with me;
but this was no girl from the huts
to be gripped and thrown aside
for a paltry coin, no absent warrior's

hungry wife. Cool as moonlight
this maiden waited on wet grass,
looking up at me with no fear, no blame,
and by her small bare feet,
panting and peeping, crouched the hare.

I saw how it would be; she'd get her land
from me, the prayer-girl, to make
a sanctuary here – and Powys
would go short of hare-meat
and the dark strong broth! I
would make my peace with the cringing dogs,
hunt forests to the north for other prey,
yet leave a thought behind me here
for her to shelter.

Cudd fi, Melangell,
Monacella, hide me!

***

Once I was Great Hare
and the Moon's companion,
and Easter's acolyte bearing the light.
Victim, I ran charred thorugh heath-fire,
lay bloodied in last corn.
I was warped to hold the soul of a witch:
dwindled to trickster and buffoon.
Men dodge my real, unchancy name,
calling me cat-shanks, cabbager,
dew-fellow, cat-of-the-furze,
maze-maker, leaper-to-hill.
False, broken is my boast of winning;
I crouch in dread of the fangs.
All I have been, am, she shelters.
"Not I", she says, "it is my Lord". But she
is what I know, soft-robed saint,
gentle one, who heard my piping cry,

Cudd fi, cudd fi, Melangell,
Monacella, hide me!

Gigant Striding

Leland, heading south for Rhaeadr
through wilderness, crossed over Claerddu,
no great streame but cumming thoroug cragges.

Between two little hills
a gigant striding was wont to wasch his hondes,
till Arthur killed him, for no reason known.

Perhaps it was just for his gigantic
striding, that diminished the moor;
his great hands commandeering the stream –

for being huge, anarchic; sharing
ancientness and threat
of the desolate land.

Claerddu, clear black. Unchanging
miles of soggy moor. Small plash
of the stream in a basin of stone.

The dwellers say also that the gigant
was buried therby, and shew the place.
A vast shadow hovers and is gone.

Cracks

In Penylan Road, Dinas Road, Pendref,
pavements are cracking. People there
grumble, but are not much perturbed
at this little encroachment of chaos.
Washing cars, weeding paths, they cherish,
as long as they may, all
controllable things, and go on
making small memories.

Pavements are cracking. The lines form a pattern
like rivers or roads on maps. Here and there
through the cracks creep small plants,
embellishments such as old cartographers
added in corners and margins –
pygmy beasts, fruits, cherubs, flowers,
to complement their hazardous projections
with forms of tenacious life.

Shapes in Ice

Ice-patterns on the window
have a formal, deliberate beauty,
like illustrations for an Argument from Design.
Now a blade of heat from the fan
begins to carve holes – a round one
through which I can see snow lying,
and now again snow falling;
and a wedge-shaped one, reminding me
of something seen on a journey, thirty years ago.

Windscreen wipers laboured. The beleaguered car
slowly jolted through an Easter blizzard
along the lakeside track; turned steeply uphill,
almost blind in whiteout, to the house Nantybeddau
on its hilltop. Outside, by the door,
lay the stone we had heard of, an arm's length
of dark snow-crusted density, wedge-shaped,
on its wider end blunt incisions
of a problematic alphabet.

I find my photographs, lay two side by side.
One is of the Nantybeddau brothers,
three old men hunched into raincoats,
sheltering in an open shed. Two
are almost smiling; the third
gazes off-right in meditative calm,
one hand abstractedly comforting
his sheepdog's nose. Huge snowflakes
fleck the foreground. Even then
these brothers lived, in their solitude,
a present that was most men's past.
Now they have moved into memory, that in its turn
fades into ultimate snows.

                    The other picture
shows the stone. Vulnerable too – to burial,
drowning, defacing, splitting, doomed
to deconstruction at the End of Things,
it has so far survived, speaking
whatever words each generation gives it.
Unliving, it belongs with the life
of men who cut that ancient message,
those who set it on the river shore
(under lake-water now), and those
who brought it up here, kept it
with a kind of pride.

The shapes blur off the warming window;
puddles trickle to the sill. I see
but will soon forget that Easter snow,
the dark stone at the foot of the wall,
the old men's living eyes, and the cold gentle hand
stroking and stroking the dog's uplifted nose.

Emblems

1. Chwefru

He liked that valley.
Old friends, we often made there
small discoveries, like the crab-apples
he would harvest at summer's end.
Too well acquainted with the mind's dark,
he might have had a sombre emblem,
not one like this I fashion from wings and light.

One hot day, high upstream,
we saw, incredulous, on a small stone
in the river, a crowded confabulation
of butterflies, heads together, folded wings
raying out, uncountable angels
on the point of a pin. Beyond, moorland
spread away into the eye of the sun.

There they went, rising in a whirligig,
fluttering into the invisibility
of huge light. I remember how his eyes
tracked them, till tears of dazzle blurred
stream and moor, and the butterflies were gone.

2. Morfa

I remember the marsh flowers,
sharp yellow, soft pink, in the wiry grass.
Crouching to pick them, we children
were lower than the reed-clumps,
could have toppled into clouds
that scudded through sky of pools.
Back of the town, hills reared,
but the Works ruled the flatlands,
beautiful grim shapes dark grey
on yellowed sky by day, and staging at night
the *son et lumière* of emerging steel.

The marsh air was unclear, a confusion
of sweet and salt, earth-exhalation and mist,
at the edge of a familiar miasma
hanging over the town. One day
we saw swans in shining progress
down a reedy channel, sailing locked
to their reflections, that wavered
with a polluted breeze.
                    Summing purity, clarity,
all that was not, the immaculate creatures
joined with our love of the place as it was.
Memory sees what the children did not,
ambivalence and taint; but keeps
all we then had, within one white image.

Olchon Valley

June has lit such a summer fire,
such a fire in the hedges! Sober hazel-leaves,
tipped orange-pink, flare out of green,
burn translucent against the sun.

Once there was lit such a towering fire,
such a fire in the valley! Those who sat,
sober hearers, by hidden hearths, flared
out of homespun and leather, out of curbed flesh,
to spirit, to power, climbing and spreading –
flame the Word lit, words fanned.

Not a flame from that conflagration
breaks out here today, not a drift of its ashes
blurs the black slopes over the valley. But a fire
that was always here at the heart of quiet
gathers us into its congregation.

Not the Pathetic Fallacy

Is it an inescapable vanity
to read speech in the valley's geometry,
see it written in Bryn Mawr's long line
clearly yet untranslatably,
like every word of the sun's decline?

No victim of pathetic fallacy,
you know what these things say
has no connection with what you feel,
can't do the weeping or praising for you,
is not concerned to preach or heal.

It's the next step that's hard to take,
try as you may to break
the illogical link, look and listen anew,
free from this notion of talk
going on all around (though not for you).

July is difficult, *Gorffennaf*,
month of completion, when you have
just outside the window a poetry
so exuberant, profuse metaphors of leaf
tumbling each over each, desperate imagery.

Content for long now with living
in shade, fertile uncertainty, accepting
mystery, why not give up the fight –
assent to that endless speech, let it cling
to the edge of perception, fading
to distant static, echo of light?

Strangeness

(There is no excellent beauty that hath not some
strangeness in the proportion. – Francis Bacon)

Certainly this is an excellent beauty,
not without strangeness. After the stumbling
down rarely-trodden rides, the last yards
forced through prickly spruce, these dark walls
suddenly rearing in the close dim glade
startle and delight. This is no longer
a house, though it keeps some of that shape.
Fern, fronding lintel, frilling wall,
has joined with stone in symbiosis.
This is a thing both made and grown.
If it outlasts the forest, it will lose
that weird fertility, shadowy dignity.
But for a while yet it yearns upward
from its hidden ground, a votive candle of dark.

Dog on the Hill

I had a dog who feared this hill.
Just where a house once stood,
by a twist of the path up to the ridge,
he would bristle, dip tail and run
all the way back down,
to be splash in the stream,
black blob by home's white walls.
I would go on up the track,
with nothing more to disturb me
than lack of breath.
              This morning at dawn
a trick of mist and light showed the open slope
with a pelt's ripple and sheen; black shelter-belt
wearing a glory; mound and rock throwing
strangest of shadows, like walls;
all about to change, all never to change.

Poor dog, poor beast with few graces,
perhaps he knew, the whole time,
whatever briefly touched my eyes
with unsustainable clear-sight;
whatever now at thinning of mist,
flattening of light, has gone back.

Words to Say

(i.m. L.B.)

I turn the diary pages to this month,
November, one hundred and forty years ago.
To the north-east, over those hills, a moor,
a house on the slope beyond; a man
plodding over a darkening desolation.
This was the first time I ever crossed
the boggy high tableland
of Rhôs Saith Maen. So it still is –
the Seven Stones deeper into peat, the miles
long and soggy, evening lights ahead
still welcome.

        A house full of children;
one girl beautiful. Next autumn he wrote
Her breathing is short; her face much flushed;
she has a most unnatural cough.
He had no need to explain his fear. By spring,
hope was thin and fading. October brought snow,
the most raging storm for years. He dreaded
November, sinking of the light.
Marianne now never quits her bed. Soon
the black grandeur of thirty mounted mourners
brought meagre consolation, being appropriate,
like the eulogy he thought fitting for this page,
private, yet ready for a future eye:
The charms of beauty, amiableness and virtue
had here met. She could not be beheld
without admiration and love.

There are other sicknesses now, and less
expansive words. November closes in. Still
of the untimely dead there is need to say
that she was happy and loved, and has gone away.

Into the Dark

(The last Roman soldier is thought to have left Wales by 400
A.D. The six people in this poem speak from points in the
uneasy years spanning that departure.)

1. Fort

I had a fancy only yesterday
that they were marching out
for the last time – perky,
but a bit ragged. Once there were fewer
of these wild lads from who knows where –
more of the real Romans. Gods!
How they would swing down the good roads!
I grant you this Roman Peace
pinches us sharply; and mercy
is a word most of them don't know –
remember poor Cradoc,
who sold the Commandant light weight?

But it *is* peace, if you take their way of it.
And who would want the tribes'
knives in the night? Some here
have daughters, too, who would cry
to see the Legion go.
The fort is busy enough; the trumpet
brisks and firms the hours. So why
do I keep dreaming of departure?

2. Leaving the Villa

I have never been back. At first
I hungered for the place. Sybilla,
our daughter, was born there;
all of us loved it,
the small villa under a hill
in the misty western land.

I knew we'd have to leave,
before Marcus told me,
one evening while Sybilla slept.
The farm was dying. Market roads
had roughened to pot-holed tracks,
and our men hung back, hearing
too many tales of plunder. Death
could pounce from any thicket,
lurk round any bend.

We're safe now, surely,
in the noise and cramp of Moridunum?
Marcus in mercy killed my dreams of home,
telling me of the changes – a corn-kiln
intruding in our long calm room, that looked
over green distance beyond the colonnade:
our bedchamber a store: the dolphin mosaic
(rustic, but always my pride) now broken.

Soon, I think, I shall forget.
Only it seems that unreality
threatens all places now, like mist
waiting its chance to swallow up the hill,
like death waiting on every road.

3. Change

Master from here, master from off,
what difference?
Rain is master,
quick shudder of bog,
rot of hoof, rot of udder.
Sun is master,
waterless craving,
swelling of tongue,
gadfly madness.
What change can be?

Change is rain after sun,
spring after winter,
young man's hand
now ruling old man's horse.
Change leads round and back
and is unchanging.
What other?

I watch my sheep
on the dark hill.
When eyes weary
or a young dog fails,
some wander.
Stumbling and broken,
or throat ripped
by the red slinker, they end
in stench, swarming, white scatter.
What change can be?

From under my ewes'
dungy draggle-tails
I squeeze the heavy milk.
The woman whirls and lumps it
to butter and soft fat cheese.
The woman hears talk of change
building like thunder.

Master from here, master from off,
what difference?
All are mastered
by hill's weather,
by body's forcing,
years' withering.
But the woman is restless.
When she asks
"What change is coming?"
I have no answer.

4. Mithraeum

Sunk into the hilltop
was the soldiers' shrine,
the temple of Mithras,
doubly forbidden to me,
a girl and native to this place.

The whole of that small hill was banned.
I would see on the ridge a light
spread faintly up, among the trees,
when some door below ground
opened for a moment.
They would climb the hill
in silent groups. Sometimes I saw
the Bull going up to die; it was said
they drank his blood.

Suddenly, they were all gone –
the fort empty, dung left to dry
in the stables, granary doors
creaking in an edgy wind.
Fear was there, shapeless and dense.
In the dark Mithraeum, open to me now,
fear again, and cold, and a huge absence.
I wished I knew an invocation
even to him, no god of mine: a prayer
for times of terror. But I was dumb
before his ashy altars,
and ran up into the sun.

5. Victim

We poured down her small throat
a drench of sleep-herb.
She gagged, but swallowed,
and still she screamed.
At last the sound
shrank to a scraping whisper,
then only her jagged breath.

After, we bound the stump
with blood-herb, fever-herb.
Three days, three nights
she was gone from us
into a darkness where
her mother bled and died
a hundred times, and flames
for ever licked and crunched
her childhood.

           Can I say
she is healed now? The dreams
come less often, and she is skilled
at her hop-and-grab journeys
from stool to pallet, or to crouch
by the patched hearth.

Surely these are the world's
last years. Our children
tear us with pity and guilt,
being sad inheritors of so little life
and so much hurt.

6. Supplication

On the altar-stone
bread of pain,
bitter cup.

I lift my hands
to the Threefold,
call down
the change, the joy.
The small cold mass-house
trembles with power.

Into this dark
I pray we go down
as into a holy well,
as into black waters
of healing.

In this ending
I pray we know
newness.

After this rending
I pray we find
wholeness.

Through this fire
I pray we leap
into peace.

from *Singing to Wolves* (2000)

Singing to Wolves

1. Llanthony

"Why should we stay here
singing to wolves?" said Llanthony monks;
and left for soft living at the daughter-house,
finding themselves unloved by the Welsh,
and jaded with beautiful desolation –
just what the first anchorites had loved,
such wildness a treasure, not to be spoiled
by intrusive felling and tilling. All
they wanted was to contemplate heaven,
and the hills (almost as high), with herds of deer
ranging their tops.
                        The tidied ruins
are a favourite summer place. On this
burning day only children have spirit
to dash under arches, burst from shade to sun,
shifting points of colour, as intense
as flowers in baskets hung in front
of the crowded restaurant.

                        One tiny girl,
dark-haired, cool in a blue dress,
stays apart; alone she kneels on grass,
in the shade of the chapter-house wall,
carefully picking daisies. Perhaps she,
who knows? in her generation will be one
whose love is given to the remote, solitary,
trackless; to risk-encircled beauty;
deer on the marches of heaven; the sweet
unprofitable singing to wolves.

2. Capel y Ffîn

The stone gives nothing but a name,
initials, dates of birth and death,
and then a verse about the sweetness,
depth, of laughing. He lies, or she,
near a line of yews, whose twisted trunks –
one pot-bellied, splay-footed, others
goat-hoofed and pitted – seem
compatible with deep, wild, joyously
contorting laughter.
                              Odd and true
this remembering; sad
the rattling laughter of survivors,
stones in the river's heat-struck bed,
rolling, falling about, denied the depths.

3. Cwmioie

So hot! Colours are soft in haze,
long tawny grass round the tombs,
brown shoulders of boys and girls
sunning by the crooked church.
Built on tiptilted rock, it leans
every which way, buttressed,
stable after its fashion, with an air
of kindly eccentricity.

Inside, in the cool, a man
lies asleep on a pew, near
the tablet to seventeenth-century
Thomas Price, who "takes his nap
in our common mother's lap",
his dust a compatible neighbour
for the bronzed and breathing sleeper.

"Better death than long languishing",
says Cadogan's motto. Amen to that,
on this day of heat and sleep,
amen! But after no long sickness
three small girls of one house came home
early from play. From their black memorial
one-year-old Mary cries "I was but young",
and claims eternal rest, being too tired
too soon.
        The sleeping man wakes up. Outside,
the sunbathers have gone. A breeze mutes heat,
scampers over the graves, and starts
a susurration of grass, not unlike
whispers or stifled laughter.

4. Merthyr Clydawg

Clodock; it sounds rustic, and English.
Clydawg; the lost Welsh is back. He seems
an off-beat martyr, killed for love,
out hunting, by a jealous rival; yet,
a prince who led in battle and prayer,
his story has a spice of miracle. Oxen
(helped by a broken yoke) refused
to drag his body over the ford, insisted
that here should be his burial-place.

In the church, the gallery's music-table
might be straight from Hardy. But Latin
on a dug-up stone remembers
"that faithful woman the dear wife
of Guinnda", who centuries back
lived in this place of shifting boundaries,
strife, loss, perpetual haunting, garbled names,
Welshness in the soil's depth,
unacknowledged riches,
uncomprehended power.

5. Michaelchurch Escley: Christ of the Trades

The mural is faded. Least defined
is the figure of Christ. He is a blaze
of pale flesh. All round him
are harder shapes, of axe-blade,
knife-blade, hammer-head, spoke, tine,
griddle-bar, saw-tooth. The blades
are turned towards him. One slanting sword
is poised by his right shoulder; its point
hovers just short of his skin. Scissors, shears
overlap the line of his arm; is he cut?
One hand, the right, presses his breast; the other
is raised, palm out – warding off, or giving
a left-handed blessing? He seems
menaced by aggressive sharpness, closing in
with intent to wound; the things of everyday
banding to shear, scrape, gash, destroy
the extraordinary. In stillness
he bears the encroachment, stands
pale on the dim wall, his body a window
letting enter invulnerable light.

Iorwerth in Cwm Pennant

They say that he, Iorwerth the blemished one,
had a refuge here, where Dafydd his brother
killed him for the lands of Arfon.

They say that if
by conquest and the death of brothers
Iorwerth had lorded it over all
their father's lands, he could not inherit
(lop-nosed from youth) the name of King.

They say that men
still held the old, merciless
dogma – marred King, weak realm;
would not have much lamented
this death in the secret valley, being used
to culling blemished beasts.

They say that all,
kneeling by taper-light at the shrine,
would own themselves blemished,
their inheritance bought back for them
by mercy; would then go out shriven, and meet
again the ancient inexorable dark.

Leah Lost

The gentle whippet, delicate
as poised courtier-dogs
in a Book of Hours, went missing.
Mad we all dashed over the road
to the Gardens. Mad we stared
accusingly at the neighbour
whose Great Dane must be,
must be the villain, for he
had gone too. Neighbour smiled
at the little dwt of a bitch
going off with a giant. Mad
we missed the joke.

In I went
to get sandals for running, searching,
through Clyne of the hundred paths;
and there she was, akip on the bedroom floor,
serene, inviolate. Back to her owner –
happy greetings, non-happening.

Along the twisting puzzle-paths,
over the red bridge, out from the trees,
wild sped the whippet-ghost
in joy, and, keeping pace,
hugely the Dane-dog. Who knows
in what world he was running,
how companioned, when back, and where found?

Unread file

This is a place left
at some undocketed moment
of ill-defined importance.
Why has my mind
pulled from a dusty shelf
this abandoned file? Here again
is that one house in a street
of tall houses; windows flaring
in low sun; shadows of leaves
shifting on the wall. A block away
there's a piano scratching up silence
with the claw of a maddening phrase
assiduously practised. There has been
no haunting, in sight or sound.
What was to be forgotten
has remained so. Only, now,
fleetingly comes that consciousness
of leaving, and flooding in
with a soft violence the sense
of what was probably pain.

Postbus

May market-day, hot as summer;
the postbus rollicks along the lanes
with a load of laughing women.
Driver's a wit, a boyo, jollies us
mile after mile. Jammed merry
in the bouncing bus, I think
how our journey would look from the sky –
a minute red insect creeping
on a grey line through green. Suddenly
I'm here and there at once. We're all
going up with exploding laughter,
shrieking, howling with glee and not caring,
tears drying in the lifting airs –
flying, flying.

Cucullatae

(Three carved figures at Housesteads are called the "Cucullati" – hooded men. The aspects of the Triple Goddess are Maiden, Wife and Hag.)

My English grandmother
is sitting on a deck-chair
at Tenby. She is draped
in uncompromising black
(she has lost her husband,
thirty-seven years ago).
Her hat is a huge
cottage-loaf, top tier
tortured with a jet pin. One sees
she is accustomed to rule.

Next to her is my mother,
also enveloped, though not
so blackly. (My father is alive,
out of frame, taking the picture).
Her dignified hat, broad-brimmed,
set straight, well pulled down, risks
a bright note – an encircling scarf.
She looks a little anxious;
judging by the direction of her gaze,
her chief worry is me.

Six years old, I sit at their feet
on the sand, bare-footed
but otherwise thoroughly
swathed, wearing a beehive hat
of indeterminate stuff,
that encases my head
from crown to eyebrows.
My faint smirk may be saying
though hitherto I have been
unempowered, that won't last.

Angel Triptych

1. Faceless Angel

Stone sword at his side, dog at his feet,
he has a small angel each side
of the stone pillow, to prop his head.
This one sits huddled up to him,
wings folded, robe in changeless folds,
slim hand just touching his mailed shoulder,
her head thrown back to gaze
imploringly upward, if she had eyes.
But the faithful have scrabbled for centuries
at her pretty face, to steal
some powdery take-away holiness.
The sculptor's image of a higher being
enduring lowly service is stronger now
by accident, faith itself having humbled
the little angel by revering her.

2. Angel and Invisible Tree

(The wooden statue of Jesse in St Mary's, Abergavenny is
thought to have formed the base of an entire missing tree, a
design for the old reredos.)

Jesse sleeps. Extruding a dynasty
has overcome him. A stump
is all that remains of the Tree.
No worm in the wood's heart
has eaten away his dream
of branchy maze, richness, sure design.
The angel at his head is awake
to see for him, so the Tree
goes on climbing, blossoming,
its boughs full of birds, people, creatures,
stories, fantastications, bunchy fruits,
extraordinary treasures. It seems to deny
nothing but death, but the angel
sees that too – the Tree cut, stripped,
planted on a black height;
and budding, sprouting again
exuberantly, looming aloft
in curly fronded complexity.
Jesse need not wake yet.
With amazement, the angel sees.

3. Angel with Wolf and Saint

The angel sits by the well
communing with a wolf and a saint.
It seems like a long
recognizing of each other.

The well is half-hidden in a stone shrine.
Steps go down to dark water;
walls are slimy, colder
than their many hartstongues.
Below the hill, in trees, is a future house;
its grey walls waver with branches seen
through them. The church, too, above the well,
is as it will be; look hard
and you may see yourself, marvelling
at its ancientness and sanctity.

The angel is kin to the wolf in his wild
innocence, troubling to man. But the saint
is more than ordinary, being holy.
He is not afraid of these beings,
though each is alien. One knows
earth, cover, hunger, mating-stench
and the blood of blameless killing; the other
lives in the eternal surprise of heaven.

All three sit quiet within
the saint's prayer, a blessing
like well-water, like the cool of leaves
wavering through walls that do not exclude.

Camarch in Sun

The afternoon was dazzle, shimmer,
a haunting in sun's dark eye.
It seemed glinting river, alder-shade,
heat-firmed mud of worsening track,
ruffling spread of old hedges,
fields below forest, still spelling
(in rich grass or thistle)
good land, bad land,
ploughed or never-ploughed,
a life's mixed fortune – all
could go, a valley vanish
at wing-flash, light-strike.
The land seemed a sojourner
no less than its people had been,
soon like them to go hence,
soon to be no more seen;
and in its decrepit beauty,
feverish with sun, pleading
a little longer to be spared.

Leasehold

Not much more of your lease to run.
So many echoes in the stones! How
does each tenancy escape them,
making its own story? When you leave,
keep something; pick one day, perhaps,
make it your emblem. I'd take
that day in June, the hawthorn year,
each hedgerow, each twisted tree
turned into fantasy by puff-balls, swags,
garlands, fountains, cataracts of white, sun
pressing out their troubling scent.
Laughter of the boy and girl lazing on grass
drifted down to the river's shade; to-and-fro
calling, snap of branches, marked where the children
were forcing a tunnel through underbrush
to the old ford. Voices were harmonics
of others, further away. Everything
was passing, in festival procession,
dancing as it went. Only, up there,
gables of house and barn, dark on hot sky,
were dense hard shapes promising
permanence. Nothing else lied.

New Telephone

All up the half-mile track,
under oaks on the verge,
in and out of gravel, fresh weeds,
twig-fragments, loose earth, stones,
old leaves blown and caught,
goes the new telephone wire.
The house is alive. Back and fore
words will dance and stumble,
check and flow.

                    The day
is heavy as unuttered threat.
No visible movement; only
the undetectable wheeling of earth
brings, this moment, a ray of dazzle
where none was. Hills upstream,
seen past huge foreground trees,
can't long be stared at,
so bright they are, and vague,
as if some transfiguration
is being enacted out of sight.

The valley's dark
slinks to black pools, or lies
a beaten beast in underbrush,
but has not died.

                    At last
a fragile wind, almost cool,
whiffles down the track –
an enigmatic hint,
like ambivalent words
waiting in the wires.

Driving Through 95% Eclipse

There was dark but not blackness here.
Behind cloud, a sliver of unseen sun
stayed, denying us that coveted extreme.
From the start, grey stretched to cover
the dull glare of an uneasy sky.

All morning the car radio gave a count-down.
Hours away from dark, miles from home,
the few cars coming towards us had lights
already. Everyone out on the road
seemed to hurry, as if a shadow
coursed at our backs and urged us on
to a shadow ahead.

Long after homecoming and the slow return
of day, some of those drivers
will have remembered speeding through
mid-morning dusk; how that near-dark
harried, then enclosed them; and how they knew,
briefly, how different is real
from ordinary, and where their wishes lay.

Llansteffan

The quicksands are further out,
by the Point. Here, there's a hint only
of that lethal instability; the beach
looks firm, but screaks and sinks
underfoot, leaving dark pits,
oddly shaped, as though the Goat-foot
has passed, under hanging woods.

Turning up past the one house that ventures
to take that shore for neighbour, up
by a tree-hung stream, I reach the well.
In its long life, later centuries
have tried to tame it – steps
down to an unceiled cell of dank stone;
St Anthony in relief on the wall;
a gothic niche for the healing water.
There is even an offering-shelf,
for pins mainly; pins for cures, pins
for love, its hope and slaking.

The wind passes through high trees,
out of control. Water is still
but feral, sister to wind, to sands
that gleam and kill, out by the Point.
Anthony had the transformer's art,
to use danger for power. Gingerly
I dip my hand. Anthony of the Well,
pray for me. I have no prayer of my own –
make one for me out of wild trees,
dark water, unstable sands.

from: Llŷn

Enlli

Faint and grey, Bardsey came out of the mist.
We could just catch, out there, what a poet saw
seven centuries back: the white waves leaping
around the holy island of Enlli.
No sound from them; the wind was too loud,
and the sea too loud, against the headland,
beating, tearing.

       That's how the island
has stayed with me, a far silence
within storm, a shadow hardly seen,
beyond the clarity of gorse on the hill,
and the blurred surging of the autumn sea.

I have never landed there; the place
remains more visitant than friend.
Why it should be so loved, though,
I can sense, unclearly, as I still see
that shape far out in spume and rain,
beyond the silent waves that leap and leap
around the holy island of Enlli.

Felling-machines

At last the spruce-trees were coming down.
Slung down the hill, taut and tense went a line
sharp against sky, and jauntily ridden
by a contraption like a little yellow
hook-armed cable-car. It went gliding down
to be loaded with roped tree trunks
and ride the sky-line, winched back up
to the growing pile of slender poles.

I thought forest-felling machines
were benign. Yet when one creature
swung again and again its ripping claw
to uptroot tree after thin tree,
I didn't want to cheer, though wouldn't have opted
for changing the outcome. These were trees
(never likeable) planted thirty years ago
to grow towards this day, to be torn up,
bundled, and take the sky-ride. I just wished
their silly bare skinny crammed-together trunks,
with the engine of death swinging again
towards them, would stop reminding me
of something human, doomed.

Polluted

Suddenly the spring, never known to fail,
ran dirty. Whatever the flaw,
it was deep in the hill.
Water came clouded from the rock,
yellow-grey from tap to glass.
Work high on the hill? – churning
of dozers and grabs? All that rain,
months of it? But this was no
earthy sediment that would settle;
the water had changed,
suffered through and through
a disquieting otherness from the norm.
It seemed the great sow of a hill
that suckled the valley-dwellers
had fallen sick, might inadvertently
feed them poison, or worse, might will
this perilous lactation, wishing them gone.
Before testing, quickly as it had come
the pollution went. Sweet water,
lucid and healthy, flowed as ever
from nourishing depths. It still runs clear.
Perhaps before long it will wash away
dregs of doubt, residual fear.

The Long Room

In Memory of John Jones, Esquire,
who by his Courage and Daring on the High Seas
and by his Industry and Thrift
(*and by the African Trade*)
paid the Debts of his Kin, and set their House
upon a Rock of Virtue and Profit.

"I don't want to sleep where I did before",
said the girl. "Thought you liked the long room, thought
you liked looking across the valley". "I did,
but not the dreams! Men and women, black, chained.
Iron and blood all through the dreams.
Couldn't get the words – not like ours. Crying, though,
there was crying. Something forcing, something afraid.
People dreamed there, and woke, and it was the same.
Iron and blood and fear".

John Jones knew human from less-than-human,
and that what can be used should be used,
and that the user may take pleasure in using.
John Jones listened to a voice in his blood, that sang:
Here is a hardness for cracking,
a softness to provoke the whip,
a brokenness to bleed under grating of chains,
a strength to sag under impossible loads,
a hole for spilling of lust,
a howling like nothing ever heard.

"You and your dreams, girl! Nothing there.
Though some say... Nothing. Go on, then,
you can have the other room. Happy now?"

So many years since the song in his blood
ended. He began to dream,
and the dream caught him.
In the long room, iron, blood, fear.
Something forcing, something crying.
He has paid the Debts of his Kin.

Neighbour

It was murky for October even on open hill,
dusk on the forestry track, night
on either hand. Below the path
was a trace of walls – Caeglas.
Dark day, dark trees conferred
a chilly mystery, estranging stone,
creating sombre shapes with little to say of home.

At night, downstream, I thought of dark on dark
in that desolation, wind getting up
with a black whirl of branches around Caeglas,
crying in crevices of rock,
ruffling noisy invisible streams,
buffeting walls, as when
there were those to hear it.

Even in this I was included,
as the same wind thrummed on my roof,
cried on my hearth, as on my dark
neighbour's; even in this.

Snow

All day snow had floated, driven, whirled,
fountaining sometimes in wild patterns
of storm's making. At evening
light from the window showed a white
insistent devil-dance, still going on.

I woke near midnight in the chair.
Film-credits were rolling past backdrop
of a steep, desolate valley, snow falling
at the end of a short day.

                    That indifferent film
must have wound to a sad ending,
unless the hollow music, dark grandeur,
were ironic comment on a glib dénouement.

Lettering dwindled to routine recording –
names of Gaffer, Grip, Best Boy.
Behind them, slowly, compellingly,
the lens travelled upstream.

                  Thicker and thicker
came the snow, obscuring black forests,
black ridges of rock. In small disturbing shifts
focus sharpened on a nearing, half-hidden
mountain blocking the valley's end.

At last, silence: all journeying blind in whiteout:
then the blank screen.

            Here, outside,
night, a blind and silent valley,
and snow falling, snow falling.

Into the Wind

1. Into the Wind

The first insecure yellowing leaves
were starting to drift free. One
landed at her feet in the sheltered yard.
"I'd sooner have the leaves", she said;
"on the hill, they get the winds".
All up the slope rose sycamore, oak, beech,
stand above stand. The small farmhouse
would soon be deep in leaves, unless this woman
tackled them each day. I imagined her
at that autumn chore, strongly sweeping
crisp leaves into great acrid fires,
never giving them the chance to slime
and blacken under sliding feet.
Later, above the farm, she sped past,
expansively waving from her dented car,
hurtling up between trees and trees,
bursting on to open road, open hill,
into the wind.

2. Bugeilyn

is farm, lake, way of life,
the handbook says. That life is cut
to an intake's few rituals. The track
is strong with a sense of destination,
but the house won't last long. The lake
is no more eternal than rock,
could go gliding in a final slide of ice,
or hiss into a gulf of cinder and flame;
but may have many millennia yet
to stretch greyly ahead, lapping
stones, muddy grass, roots of a tree,
when wind flicks it shorewards.

The day has been dull as locked-up fear;
now sun pierces it, wind leaps up,
rippling lake blazes white. We choose to take
the onward track, its damp stones shining,
towards the shore, house that has been,
transient overpowering glory.

3. Matrix

It looks an old landscape.
Centuries back, as now, there would have been
grey-brown moor, horizon mountain,
sliver of blue far over on the right –
the lake one day to be called Glaslyn,
for the way it catches and holds any scrap
of cerulean brightness. The youngest thing
is the track, laborious embodying
of a quick thought that leapt towards the hills.

Eastward, once into leaden Dylife
life poured; bleak seasons wheeled
and it drained away. Now, scars, relics,
phthisic ghosts. Further, Carno way,
mist parts and closes, intermittently showing
shapes on the ridge that gleam and whirl,
distance and trick of light, kind to their strange
proportion, making them earthfast seraphim.

In the old landscape with its dark moor,
blue lake under the mountain's bulk, for long
little traceable has happened. Yet it seems
to lack nothing, deny nothing; rather
to include, as white light holds all colours,
the virgin bears the god.

4. The Petticoat

After the lead-mine came, the stream
was known as Nant-y-Barracks. Along it
the track now led to a stark hut
with double row of narrow beds,
dingy shirts limp on hooks,
grubby scuffed floor.

On the way up, across the stream
was the one house for miles.
Sometimes a bony thin-haired woman
would be spied, scurrying in
with an armful of peats, or heard
screeching to her dog.
The girl was kept close.

                    As they passed,
the miners eyed clothes hung to dry,
like the slender red petticoat
one day strung in the sneaky wind,
that sleeked it, turned, teased,
entered it; then, round the sour
shut-in maleness of the barracks
mockingly whinnied and snickered all night.

5. Hyddgen

They still use the pens
and long grey sheds. Distantly,
over the moor, we see a huddled gather
of flocks, some human figures, too far
for any eye but the mind's to catch
the wrestle and plunge to the dip, frenetic scramble,
shoving into order. Red burly men
who seem to have feasted on desolation
will be jostling with wiry ones, shrewd faces
lined with endurance and laughter.

No woman of the house to joke with them,
spread heavy lavish food. The house is gone,
after long holding of hard life; last
a haunting of light, shining at dusk
from empty windows.

We climbed high to get here,
labouring car zig-zagging up
a forestry road to the Bwlch,
bumping over the plateau. Pumlumon
looms over boggy acres.
Carn Hyddgen lifts twin cairns
on the eastern sky.

               "Can you hear it?"
asks one, and yes, it's there,
that almost-silence, not quite hum,
not quite drone, so very faint,
the voice of the land when nothing intervenes;
too far away, too deep within
to be understood, but never sounding
like language of elegy or ending.

New Poems

Not Heaven, Perhaps

Heading for Cardiff, the train passes a spot
I try not to miss –
a glimpse of red roof,
and the dark spread of pine
I used to climb into.
Then it all rattles away.

It's been years since the poplar
disappeared. That grew next door,
thin, startlingly tall. Seen
from our attic it rose higher still,
topped by a long twig that might seem
to indicate aim or destination.
Not heaven, perhaps –
celestial blue easily and often
dimmed into grey, tranquillity
turned to rock and scud of storm.

An accident of woody growth,
high-rising sap, pointed year after year
at a firmament of risk.
But the child I was, free of compulsion
to translate shape as message,
saw slenderness, leafiness or starkness,
dizzy tallness; dived upwards into blue,
skimmed across the moon,
towered into thunderheads, saw
too much to interpret, knew
too much to forget.

Skirling

In Wales, we would call it an *allt*
(I didn't know what it was
in the cousin language) –
woods covered the hill
from rocky shore to summit crags.
Each time I walked by the sea
the beach was empty, but from somewhere
midway up the slope, secret in trees,
came the sound of bagpipes.
"Skirl" – a word I remembered;
was it the right one for this
solitary music? It was an ancient sound,
strange to me in its isolation,
echo-less thinness, jaws-to-tail
convolution.
　　　　　　When I left the beach
it stayed behind, endlessly infiltrating
waves' hushing, softly-blown sand,
quiet rush of rain on rock;
so that I can't rerun that memory
without its incidental music –
far up in dark trees,
above rocks and western sea,
insistent, a small high skirling.

Wind-chimes

Sometimes I wake
just as I'm walking in.
I can't get used to the way
the house vanishes then.
Waking, I can get it back,
but that's a willed thing,
not the return sleep can give
generously, sometimes.
The will disciplines, insists
the house shall be empty;
nothing hides patches,
stains, mouldy bulges.
Windowsills are naked
of plants, windows
of curtains. The huge porch
between kitchen and yard
has no row of graded boots,
no sagging dog-box, hutches,
muddy coats. Everything looks
as it did when the story began,
and the day it ended.
There are no voices; only
wind-chimes on the back wall
escape the censor. Still
they make their non-human music
of change and no-change, music
seeming, now as it always did,
to hold an undersong of regret.

Bereft

(i.m. R.S. Thomas)

Now is the time
of the dark house,
the empty shore.
Now the argument
is between us, unaided,
and the great Absence.
We have lost the one
who had words to catch
a wordless resonance.
We have lost his sharp cuts,
his logic's elegance.
He is not to be found
by black hearth, bare altar.
Vainly we search for him
in the processions
of sea-creatures at their mass,
and in the sky-wide whir
of the migrations.
Bereft, we cling
to his image of mercy
in crevices of rock,
to the hope of finding,
as he did one day, the meaning
of a sombre landscape
in a single sunlit field.

Pictures of Zeugma

They have so little time.
An archaeologist lovingly wipes
the last smears of dirt from opening eyes
of mosaic images, blinded for centuries.
Daedalus, Icarus, Pasiphaë,
rich colour swirling, wake to enchant her.

Glued, bound, cut in sections,
they are carried off, saved.
While days, hours, remain
there can be no lamentation,
only controlled frenzy of rescue.

A small boy watches appalled
his father smashing their house
into useful fragments. What they can
they will save; somewhere else, rebuild,
try to forget the inundated life,
lorries leaving, weeping women
bundled aboard.

                        Slowly
the lake fills. Fragments of wall
fold into flood. "I am bitter",
says the leader of the dig,
as the lost villas, so many, still
underground, shut from sight,
are yielded up to water.

Children from the high slopes
run down to a new shore, skim stones,
point at tilting rooftops out there
like fins cutting water. On the lake-bed
mosaic dancers, flowers, leaping beasts
from two thousand years ago
flicker unseen over drowned floors
as the mud-shroud loosens.

A truck-ride away, the boy
watches a new house grow.
He picks up a chunk of wood,
copies the hammering.
Sometimes in sleep he sees
falling walls, light losing itself
down a staircase of water.

Letters from Briga

Claudia Severa asks Lepidina
to her birthday party,
sends greetings from Aelius
and their little son; ends with
Vale, soror, anima mea karissima –
Farewell, sister, my dearest soul.

Again, still at Briga,
telling her plans (worn away
from the fragment of tablet),
she sends a valediction –
Farewell, my sister,
my dearest, my most longed-for soul.

The Latin is stately,
patterned. But the voice
on a north wind from Briga
speaks love. *Soror karissima*
et anima desideratissima...
Farewell, sister, farewell, my dearest soul.

Threat

(A found poem from letters of 1847.)

Thomas Lewis, I have heard
that you will give your daughter
to an idle evil man
and put her on the unjust lands
of Trewern Fach.

You are a proper fool
to give the outwitted wench
to the roguish thief-man.

I will send up to you
the Servant's Daughters.
They will burn all you occupy
and your daughter to it.

I pity the poor people
who paid four hundred pounds
and upwards for the land.
You now maliciously combine
and steal it back for nothing.

Thomas Lewis,
I will take care of you.

Yours most affectionately,
Rebecca.

Pig

One pouring evening on holiday
the heaters failed; we bundled
the children in blankets.
The landlord arrived, bearing no fuel,
but in the mood for a chat. For an hour
he told us stories of pigs, their charm,
their niceness, their more than human
intelligence, the balance they keep
between reason and rich intuition.

We heard of the pig in a pub,
obstinately waiting for his pint
to be pulled and presented;
the family pig, friend of children;
the nest-building sow, who took to the hills
to farrow, first bringing her master
a twist of grass, bracken, rush,
for a clue to her destination.

More than pig-stories, it was his total
pig-devotion that struck us.
It was over-the-top, like the weather out there,
like our situation – cocooned children,
dank room with miles of rainy desolation
beyond its walls. After he left,
heaters clicked on; ordinariness returned.
Years later, rain and a cold room sometimes
remind me of hairy camphorous blankets,
long-bodied metallic bristliness of pig.

Under the Road

Under this road run spindles and gears
of an old technology. Here's where
the water-wheel linked with the barn
to power chopping and mangling,
crushing, snipping and squeezing.
They didn't bother to dismantle
the obsolete contraption, just threw
on top of it a stony porridge
of rough road, smoothed it over.
Things seem better that way.
Something in our make-up senses the bang
of Armageddon, whimper of world-plague
could be more than fantasy; hopes
we'd struggle up from slough or desert,
learn it all again. I can see the sharp one,
the pioneer, fingering the puzzle
he's dug from churned-up ground.
Step by step he'll work it out,
try his avant-garde system. In no time
there'll be wheels whirring in the barn.
The covering road is decades,
centuries ahead.

Bantam on Straw

Gold, cream, black, red
the bantam stalks
in miniature grandeur
on the disinfectant mat.
Disarranging scarcely
one wisp of damp straw
he lifts one claw, then the other,
high, circumspectly,
slightly nodding his crest.

It's as if I'm remembering this
from the earlier time. But no,
all that stayed with me
after '67 was miasma,
a gone-off barbecue smell,
worry like a smothered scream.

Something dateless
is what I'm seeing now –
more than indifference,
a built-in unknowing
in the way things are.
Yet there's this lift of the heart
at the sight of the small grandee,
a creature hardly less other
than grass that after a while
covers, and seems to restore.

Voices

From down the road come faint goodbyes,
the sound of cars leaving.

Distant booming from the Range
brings with it a tiny judder.

The house absorbs it, renews
a limited promise of safety.

Cries of buzzard and kite can mean
freedom or savagery;

only the ripped victim's minute shriek
is unambivalent.

Cries

(i.m. Thomas Cairns, d. 1871, aged 12)

His first cry
was thin but angry
as the midwife dangled him,
thumping air in, forcing out
that reedy protest. Yet it's a cry
I never heard him voice
that sounds in my head.

As a boy
he was always off to go, rushing,
stretching, scrambling, balancing.
He'd be first to know
where peregrines nested, or how
fox had given hounds the slip.

If he was tired for once,
or some childish sickness
kept him by the fire,
he would lean against me,
half asleep; never for long.

The day he fell
was loud with a gale
that ripped at cliff-side trees
below our platform of hill.
Tearing along, he must have tripped
at the edge, hurtled straight down.
The rocks broke him. No-one knows
if he died fast.

I know he screamed,
because at times, night or day,
I hear him.
Once in a while, by the fire,
he leans against me, quietly;
then off to go, never mind the storm –
off to go.

Fields of Force

1. Dancer

By the Lodge, the road
curls past a shrubbery
that even at noon
never forgets night,
tall fir-trees, thick bushes
combining to hoard the dark.
One glade is open to sky.
There, once, a woman would dance
in transports of full-moon madness,
round rhododendrons,
through wet grass or summer dust,
reeling, stumbling, righting herself,
off again in her wheeling and whirling,
till clouds came, or dawn,
to take away the galvanic light
that was her frenzy, ecstasy, power;
leaving her slumped, grey, sloppy-slippered,
anti-climatic, tired, tired.

2. Mare

In a green meadow of increase
the mare was usually alone;
sociable, though, or greedy,
ambling to the gate in hope of an apple.
The stallion they brought her
was nondescript, but she
was set alight. She frisked;
it seemed she coquetted,
the way she bumped shoulders
and dashed away, head turned,
shaming him into following. He
caught some of her grace and elation.
They sped along the riverbank in the sun,
as through a force-field, borrowing power.
She's in foal now. Alone again,
she plods to the gate, nosing for apples.

3. Chapel

Ninety years ago
the chapel was pulled down.
At each corner of the site,
as remembrance of walls,
roof, wholeness, life,
they planted, as was the custom,
a tree. It was as if
in this place there was still
something needing years to grow,
slowly, slowly reaching up;
as if all the prayer and singing,
all the love and observance,
had to have somewhere to go;
as if those who come even now
to trace names on stones,
rest on the new seat,
speculate, contemplate, weep,
must know, in breathless weather,
the shade of a rooted power.

4. Question

Bronfelen, tawny hill –
was there a house here?
None now. Nothing known.
Only the blaze of the hill –
red-brown bracken in autumn,
red speckling thin white of December,
residual red under new green fronds
in the growing year.
A boundary zone
between known and known;
a place of blurred identity;
an acreage that's lost
the filaments tying it once
to something recognisable,
unique, to things lived
and for a time remembered. Still,
now and again, people ask
"Was there a house here?"
as if something scattered might
cohere, some force be acknowledged,
some elusive meaning might find
its irrefutable words.

Lunar Eclipse

The earth is up there –
that's how it seems; shrunken
but solid, aggressive, black-red.
The shadow is here,
these insubstantial fields, barely-seen
creep of the stream.

           The earth-shape
is dragging itself up, slowly, slowly,
over a huge weak moon.
It has clawed and clutched its way
to dominance.
           Tales are forgotten
the shuttle-crew told, of soft earth-light,
tranquil, blue. A predator-planet
now shows itself as it is,
blood-dark, dangerous.

Yet soon the silver rim
reappears, the sliver of hope.
Slowly, slowly the leeching blackness
dwindles, slips down.

              Earth
is again these fields, this river.
The shape that had seemed no shadow
has vanished between the stars, become
an ambivalent memory, diffused
in the light of an intact moon.

Stones

1. Third Face

Late sun sharpens green
of pleached limes by the path
from churchyard gate to porch,
yet softens blue of wooded hills
over the deep valley.
There was a stonemason here
who loved cherubs – just their faces,
fat and oddly sour, their mouths
downturned, perhaps in grief?
Or did their carver sense,
issuing out of the mouths of babes,
bleak wisdom on mortality?

Two cherubs ornament a stone
patterned with lichen, obscure lettering.
A curling line springs up to make
a rough cartouche for the round heads
and something else, fainter, smaller,
darker grey – a third face, just
perceptible, emerging or receding,
like someone never fully there,
a stillborn sibling or a child
silent and self-estranged all its few years,
who now is part of this late day,
with low sun, woven trees, dim lines on stone.

2. Llanvetherine Angel

Asymmetrically set, lurching
across a tombstone, is a strange version
of a celestial being. He looks drunk
or a little mad. Perhaps the carver
tried for divine frenzy; all he managed
was this ungainly angel, who blears
at one splayed hand, seeming to count
his pointy fingers as reassurance
for a distraught mind.

                                Lettering
has worn away, lichened stone
has flaked. Nothing remains to speak
judgement or love, forgiveness, praise;
there's not the coldest record cut to last.
Only this half-crazed angel
has flapped in from the edge of a world
and stayed, a voice for the silent,
opening the niminy o of his mouth
to utter a constricted cry.

3. Inscriptions

a. Caeo, 6th Century

We look back, we treasure.
This was a man of gravitas,
a true inheritor.
We must remember, we must copy, we must transmit.
Shadows are background to rational light.
We do not recognize the dark
beyond these bounds. All shall be fittingly done.
Thus we remember noble Paulinus –
A guardian of the faith,
always a lover of his homeland,
here Paulinus lies,
most conscientious observer
of all that is right.

b. Llanlleonfael, 7th Century

Were there certainties in the old time? We inch
forward through dusk toward a ground of trust.
Around the warriors' stone, shadowy changes dance.
Boundaries shift, waver. Nothing is constant,
nothing clearly seen. A new thing grows
from a forgetting. Thus we name
two who wait for the judgement of light –
Silent, enshrouded,
Iorwerth and Ruallaun
in their graves
await the dread coming
of the Judge, in peace.

Omen

We washed the bloodied rags
to use again and again
as my father coughed his way to death.

One night my mother and I
saw the funeral lights.
All down the track from our yard gate
the lantern-line, dwindling, dipped and swung.
In mid-procession twin brightnesses,
a gap of dark between,
marked where the horse-bier journeyed,
carrying him away.
                              My mother wept.
I coaxed her in, saying
we must make his broth.
Within a week he died.
A black file of neighbours and kin
followed the predestined path.

It was the same, months after,
when my mother gave up
her tired struggle – first lights
going down into the valley's dark; soon
the quenching of her will to stay with me.

I have been alone two years,
with little help from those
who, it seems, crowd here only
for that churchward trudge.
But I am strong, hardly coughing at all
except when the corpse-wind blows. Then
there is a taste of blood.

Three nights ago
from the window I thought I saw
a gleam of lights on the track,
but pulled the curtain over,
slapped warmth into my limbs,
stirred the grudging fire, promised myself
change of wind, early Spring.

from: Riding the Flood

1. Investment

I must have given something to that day,
that bit of seeing, living; or how,
after so many years, could so trivial
a recollection yield such riches?
It's like investing a small sum
and long afterwards enjoying
the surprise of profit.
                    I remember
the steep dip of road to harbour,
houses with whitened steps, but chiefly
the waterfront café, red plastic making
a hot day hotter. Mixed with our coffee
were motorboat smells, oily, metallic, hot.

That was the rainiest of rainy towns;
yet instead of a grey memory I've kept
one fiery day. Perhaps what I gave it
was just the feeling that most things lay ahead,
and some (enough) would probably be good.

2. Riding the Flood

There are days when waves of unremembered life
tumble in, one upon another, almost
irresistibly. You can feel the thuds
through the soles of your feet, through blood and bone,
all the channels and sluices of the body.
If the sea-wall gives, houses and a host
of little, loved, scruffy gardens will be drowned,
stay endlessly soggy and salt. Best
have your boat ready, furbish your skills
in navigation, submit to being lifted
higher that you could have imagined,
ride the flood, voyage to countries
you had given up hope of revisiting. Don't ask
whether that high tide of remembering
will ever carry you home.

Legacy

Autumn brings again
cream sprays of knotweed blossom,
beautiful pest, layer on layer,
lavish on my riverbank.
"Cut it back and back", I'm told,
"it'll be discouraged – may return,
but weaker each time". Not mine –
fibrous juicy stems are tougher each year.

Upstream, none of it – conscience-stricken,
I have searched in vain. But down-valley,
by the pool under the alders
where our children would star-float
in the hot summers, I see
knotweed stragglers from my bank
massed into luxuriance.

Further down, the Irfon curves away
towards forests on the hill. Far across
water-meadows, diminishing clumps
of flowering knotweed flaunt, against
the dark of hardly less alien spruce,
their dubious exuberance – undiscouraged
succubi, my sinister, unwilled,
spectacular legacy.

Replaying

Even the bulky space-suit
couldn't quite rob her of grace.
On the way to the shuttle,
among the men, she trod
springily, as if already
breaking the shackles of gravity.
Not yet helmeted, she turned
as she walked her last of earth,
dark hair swinging, and waved – the happiest,
most understated of farewells.

After the heavily-weighted numbers
of countdown, the roar of downward flame,
the leap into the sky,
came the unbelievable fireball.

Some transgalactic venturer, one day
rummaging among records, may run this film
and surprise himself by replaying
the bit where she turns and waves.

Unhealed

At the spa, what water!
Hopeful guests by the score
pushed at the gates of health.
The spa is remembered still; those
who knew the house at its heart
read their own sadness
into its dereliction,
felt its crumbling as pain.

Long before, in forgotten years
when the spring was no more
than a stench in a nook of the lawns,
the old proud house by the river
ruled its obscure estate.
Lands were to be joined to lands.
The marriageable daughter cried,
but obeyed. Bedded by a drunken boy,
she gave him no son, knew
no healing. Here she died,
leaving two small wailing girls.

Now the house is clamped
in a brace of struts and scaffolding.
Mountain ash has been prised,
living, from a chimney. Flaking paint
is being scoured, mould confronted,
the physical sicknesses of the house
diagnosed, prescribed for, treated.

What is forgotten cannot be healed.
It hides quiet through the bountiful days;
in time of decay cries again,
an unphysicked, irremediable pain.

The Cynog Man

(Cynog, 5th-century saint and martyr, was the illegitimate eldest son of King Brychan, who gave him a gold bracelet or crown. Cynog's reputation was that of a derided Fool of God. Centuries later, till 1823, Defynog people marked his day by paying a derelict to be "gŵr Cynog". He would endure a day of mockery and be thrown into the river.)

Hey, hey, the man of God!
King's bastard with his father's gold-
bracelet or crown? Let the scholars
frippet and froth. They know
less than we, whose own dear saint
we make again one day a year
to mock and goad and mortify.
This is our veneration, our love.
Why else after thirteen hundred years
drag him back? Why think of him?

Who shall be the Cynog man
on Cynog Monday? Dummy-drunk,
urchin, simpleton, tramp,
the river's waiting – chuck him in
to splutter and choke, drip and soak,
sink or swim, the Cynog man.

Hey, hey, the holy fool!
Instead of his father's gold he crammed
an iron crown on his lousy locks,
dressed in tatters, dossed in a cave.
No seemly prayers in the churchmen's tongue –
gaunt on the rocks, he howled to God.
Some called it upside-down pride, that got him
only lean belly, cold bed, mockery.
To remember our saint, to bring him back,
we mock, we goad, we mortify.

Who shall be the Cynog man?
No sleek lad with upturned eye,
no plump and prating priest will do,
only a wreck, a no-hope sot,
to mock and goad and mortify,
as year by year we bring him back,
our saint reliving his humbling pain.
He won his crown, and us our chance,
and wins them still, our Cynog man.

Guerinou

(Guerinou is the ancient form of Grwyne. The conjoined rivers
of Grwyne Fawr and Grwyne Fechan eventually flow as one
into the Usk. Patricio, with its holy well below the church, and
old house of Tŷ'n-y-Llwyn nearby, lies on the western side of
the Grwyne Fawr. The ambush of the Norman lord Richard de
Clare took place on the eastern side.)

1. Patricio 2001

They have been bringing offerings
to the dark well, tying
rags to twigs in supplication, leaving
flowers to wilt in that chipped glass
uneasily perched on a dank ledge,
making crosses from bits of stick.

There seem so many of them, despite
the hiddenness of the place; as if
in a time of fear and shattering
these humble shapes are once more
valid – raw letters spelling out
helplessness, not yet
reshuffled into words of power.

2. Tŷ'n-y-Llŵyn

Can any day as hot and silent as this
have no darkness of doubt?
The watch on my wrist tells one time;
the disc-harrow, rusty in long grass
by the blurred path, confuses the issue,
looking obstinately recoverable.

Inside yard-gates the chaff-house
has a tree growing through it. Stable walls
are strong, but inside them
my camera-flash wakes from blackness
racks and stalls in a tilting pattern of ruin.

I come closer to the ancient house,
slowly, afraid now of finding it dead –
hopeful at topiary still roughly trimmed,
the small lawn mowed not too long since;
but wary of nettles thrusting across the steps
and saddened by the only sound, the dull
echo-less thud of my unanswered knock.

Across the valley wooded hills,
silent too, climb to a glaring sky,
Here, a stony track drops sharply down
from this shelf of land towards
an unseen, unheard river.

Something just visible at a high window
might be a jug of flowers. I look back
and think it's illusion. Yet gradually
the house makes felt a reassurance
of life not ended but in abeyance –
within silence, songs;
within stillness, running feet,
corners turned, doors flung wide,
the whirl of time funnelling down again,
filling the rooms.

From the narrow terrace
one white butterfly dances out
across the valley.
The sun's eye stares,
and the white speck is gone.

3. Incident in Vengeance Wood

In the Bad Pass of Grwyne
silence: no wind in tall trees:
no stir in dark underwood.
Then, high up, one bird calls,
like a human cry.
      In a while
clinking, jinking, hoof-pad, voices.
Stones rattle on the downward path.
A song rises, and scraping of strings –
lightly stepping, Richard de Clare's
two music-boys; he following,
lofty on a black horse.
       Snapping of twigs,
swishing of leaves. All at once
shock of ambush – vengeful bellowing,
yells of hate. Death sneaks quietly
inside the din-arrow in throat, knife
slinking swiftly to heart.
       Swish of leaves,
crack of twigs, then silence. The singer's mouth
leeches to bloodied earth. No wind
in tall trees, no stir. Then, far away,
high up, one bird calls,
like a last cry.

4. New Houses

Upstream, forestry
closes in. Allow for that.
Allow for a grey day, currents
of thundery air. Even then –
how could anyone chasing a dream
imagine that here it might be
happily captured? Unease
is spelt in the odd proportions
of a cottage, the way a house
down there by the river
suddenly looms.

Centuries back, the valley
was already feared. Surely all that
was long enough ago for hate
to have seeped away like the blood
of slaughter in those dark woods?
But slowly, slowly, inch by inch only,
the valley creeps towards peace.

Perhaps those who dream, who come here
and build, loving the place,
are carried unknowing within
that infinitesimal advance?
It seems that stone and wood have their own
knowledge; as if here houses they form
can do no other than disturb,
embodying a warning that safety
may still be a long way ahead.

5. Macnamara's Mistress

(At the turn of the 18th-19th centuries John Macnamara of Llangoed would ride over the Black Mountains on a bridleway that became known as "Macnamara's Road", to visit a mistress he kept at The Hermitage in the Grwyne Fechan valley.)

When at dusk the first flakes
blew past my windows, I was sure
this was only a flurry, a small whiteness
on the tops, a flutter of chill
he would feel on his face as he rode
over the high pass. But soon
snow whirled too fast, too densely
for hope.
             I had heated wine –
not too heavy a hand with the spices,
he taught me, just a sweet-sharp
titillation.
             She's prettyish, his wife.
Does he take what offers?
Some say she loves only land,
that she rules like a man
their opulent acres. Some say
that's all he wants of her.
I wish I believed them.

I woke to white wastes, aching eyes, cold bed.
How long till the pass clears?
He is what defines me.
Today I'm no-one. Nothing in me
can call him. I see her
pouring his wine. Snow
obliterates me. It's as if
there's no story of me, as if nobody
will ever make one.

The day ticks on.
Pressed to frigid panes
I stare into snow. I'm snow-blind,
snow-mad. Reaching for wine
I lift the glass to my eyes,
letting hot colour change
that lonely white; then drink, pour, drink.

Flickering through branches,
faintly at evening my house-lights
signal to empty hills.
Dregs of wine spatter the floor
as I sag into black sleep.

6. The Hermitage

The valley's alive. Farms work. The small road
has no grass down the middle. Hedges
sit back obediently.
                          The strangeness
may be bred of morning mist;
out of it loom steep round hills that seem
closer than the map shows.
Slinking away from them, the road
enters tall dark of trees and dips
to crisp chatter of water on stone.

Some houses create an illusion
of shunning capture, like live things
adept at camouflage.
Over the river a patch of deeper dark
becomes a fragment of wall, a window
is light between boughs.
                          Without fully
knowing why, we have come miles
in search of a broken house, unsure
who built or named it, obsessed
with an idea of hiddenness,
an unreliable story.

All too appropriately, the bridge has gone;
there's only the stumble and slither now
of a wide ford.
                          We reach our prey,
quiet at its hunters' mercy, a house
more elegant in dereliction
than we'd supposed, more unapproachable
than anyone could have planned.

As long as we can, we stay
wandering over fields that once were lawns,
peering through doorways and window-spaces,
through floorless hall to cellar,
seeing trees through undesigned
arches, guessing where stairs had climbed,
where corridors had run.
                              To imagine
presences, echoes, would seem
presumption. Structures, tangible,
broken, are speech enough.
                              As we drive away
mist clears; the valley's caught
into shining air.

7. G.F.L.R.

(The Grwyne Fawr Light Railway, which enabled a dam to be built high up that valley, never rated a Railway Act. It was considered impossible to build and run.)

Miles away along the valley
they could catch the creaky breath,
tinily growing, of the engine
battling impossible gradients
to reach the workings. A dam
in these high solitudes had seemed
fantasy. The railway never achieved
official identity, governmental
blessing. Labouring up rails
with sleepers laid on the road,
the engines huffed and groaned,
dragging incredible loads of stone
or coaches full of Grwyne navvies –
bearded Irish, a scatter of local lads.

The parenthesis in the valley's story
lasted less than twenty years.
Then the engines chugged away,
lines were ripped up, the workmen's village
dismantled. It was as though that strange life
had never come to Grwyne, as though
no children had chanted their tables,
and shoved each other in the playground;
no couples had loved in the makeshift houses;
as though late-coming conifers had always
choked the mid-valley with dark and silence.

I have no arts of conjuration,
and wouldn't want to raise this valley's ghosts.
But once, perhaps, it might be good to catch
faintly, from very far, the growing sound
of climbing engines.

Come, Dukinfield,
unstable but dauntless, cling to the rails
on the giddy gradients.
Come, trim Anita,
stay trusty on the mail-run morning and night.
Come, little Brigg,
beaten by a blizzard, try again.
Come, splendid Abertillery One,
Abertillery Two,
heavily bouncing on too-light rails,
flaunt your fluted chimneys,
your touches of copper and brass.

When it all ended, it was as though
green engines, red-buffered, had never amazed
children of the farms; as though
shrilling of whistles, crescendo
of effort, hiss of halting
had never changed the pattern of sound
shifting over ancient silence.
But in the upper valley's wilderness
rises the functional grandeur all this was for –
the dam, remote and massive. Beyond
stretches the lake, once in a while
blue under great sunny skies, oftener
caught into grey of rain that feeds it,
soaking the mountain wastes of Guerinou.

Yard in Winter

Down there the February lands
are blue, blue-green, twig-brown,
with squares and lozenges of snow.
Here, the ground's all white,
except where highest slopes
have caught the wind, that's left them
speckled with old bracken's rust.

The tilted bumpy yard is a theatre
of the inconsequential.
Three blanketed horses
turn their rumps this way
and stare towards the view.
By the house, a sandy lurcher
droops apathetically.
Across the yard, a sable greyhound
heads firmly, elegantly
for nowhere in particular.
Two men, next to each other, pursue
separate tasks. One ferrets
in the boot of a car, the other stoops
over a vertical stick, as if
testing the depth of snow. Nothing
relates to anything else.
The nondescript red house
has no visual bond with its barn –
old, grey and handsome.

What is it these distances below,
hills climbing behind, confer on a scatter
of little sights and happenings?
Not exactly meaning. What comes
is willingness not to ask for that –
a sort of gratitude: a sort of love.

The Odd Field

"That field's an odd shape!" A touch
has flicked up on the lap-top
a landscape none of us has seen.

It's not quite strange.
Hills are the same, rivers
have held their course. But on the screen
roads have turned back to tracks
that old exigencies compel
to struggle up slopes abandoned now,
to curl along old boundaries.

The odd field is a couple of boxes
joined to a long thin strip. We stare,
baffled. "Why that shape? Try going back."
The next map wakes an even earlier world;
and there's the answer. That blob
is a house on one small garth,
its garden fills the other. The skinny field
is no field at all, but a lane.

Finding this is a pleasure
almost like a happiness, or perhaps
hope-against-hope – more, certainly,
than fat contentment of a puzzle solved.
Something to do with the squudge of boots
in a muddy lane, and the way
life has of being everywhere,
then, always, now, again.

Thirteenth Gate

There were thirteen gates here once
in five miles; only the last is left.
"Why is thirteen unlucky?" – "It's not.
Thirteen is twelve, and one to make the meaning".
I can't remember finding the answer strange.

Thirteen gates. Laborious halts,
heavy cart creaking, checked again;
stamping protest of hooves,
jingling, snorting, trundling through,
click-slam of metal and wood.

At each start a new stretch to face
of stony rutted road, mud-slough
or dust-cloud, slither of ice,
choke of snow. Catkins or fall of leaf,
quiet water alongside or brown flood
spilling out. Landslip to clear,
or tumbled branches. The white still road
of summer; sudden black above,
rip of lightning, frightened horse
wrenched back into control.

Twelve gates passed. A shimmer
on the road now, a blur
of echoes and shadows. The thirteenth gate:
Hawk Hill, hill of oakwoods,
gate to the mountain road.

How to sum a journey, how value it,
till it ends? Something
is completed here, defined,
at the end of the gated road.
                              Ahead
a small wind flicks hill grass, the way
opens towards far summits.
Twelve gates are passed. Now one,
one will make the meaning.

Acknowledgements

Acknowledgements are due to the editors of the following publications where these poems first appeared:

Newspapers and Magazines:
Anglo-Welsh Review, Aquarius, Bananas, Candelabrum, Country Life, Country Quest, Countryman, David Jones Journal, Express, Independent, Interchange, Interpreter's House, Kilvert Society Magazine, London Welshman, New Welsh Review, Planet, Poetry Nation Review, Poetry Scotland, Poetry Wales, Roundyhouse, Scintilla.

Anthologies:
Anglo-Welsh Poetry 1480-1980, Between the Severn and the Wye, Birdsong, A Book of Wales, Borestone Mountain Awards, Burning the Bracken, The Calling of Kindred, Celtic Christian Spirituality, Celtic Verse, Christmas in Wales, Dragon's Hoard, Footsteps, The Hare that Hides Within, Love from Wales, Masks of Love, The Mountains of Mourne, Over Milk Wood, Poems '71, '74, '76, Poetry Book Society Supplement, Poetry Wales 25 Years, Sestet, Speak to the Hills, Thoughts Like an Ocean, Twentieth Century Anglo-Welsh Poetry, The Urgency of Identity, Wales in Verse and *Poetry Wales* cassette.

'Hoofprints' appeared as the epigraph to 'Footprints in Stone' by Janet Bord (2004).

Poems have been read on BBC Radio 3,4, and Radio Wales.

'The Long Room' was a *Roundyhouse* second prize-winner.
The first version of the sequence 'Riding the Flood' was a *Scintilla* (Long Poem) third prize-winner.

Thanks are due to David Tipper, 'Stone and Steel in the Black Mountains', which helped bring to life for me the Grwyne Fawr Light Railway.